HAUNTED INNS OF SURREY

By Roger Long

Also by Roger Long

MURDER IN OLD BERKSHIRE 1990
I'LL BE HANGED 1991
THE CROWTHORNE CHRONICLES 1992
HAUNTED INNS OF THE CHILTERNS AND THAMES VALLEY 1993
FINAL COMMITMENT 1994
ANCIENT BERKSHIRE INNS AND THEIR STORIES 1996
HAUNTED INNS OF HAMPSHIRE 1999
CAESAR'S CIRCLE 2000
HAUNTED INNS OF SUSSEX 2001

1st edition published September 2002

ISBN 0 9534735 4 6

Published by: Conservatree Print and Design, Reading, UK
Printed and Bound in Great Britain.

Publisher's Note

Whilst every care has been taken to ensure the accuracy of all the information contained in this book neither the author nor the publisher can accept responsibility for any mistakes that may occur.

Photographs: Brenda Allaway
Compilation: Dave Blackman

FOREWORD

I did not quite know where to start with *Haunted Inns of Surrey*. Firstly, I had no intention of going very far into what is really sub-urbian London, the north-eastern third of the county. Whereas my previous books on haunted inns in Berkshire, Hampshire and Sussex have clear boundaries, Surrey (proper Surrey) is far less definable.

I was a little disappointed in towns like Kingston and Reigate as far as haunted pubs are concerned. There is a plethora of old inns in both towns but not a shade of a spook in any of them. Redhill is now gutted in every sense of the word and Woking never did have many pubs to speak of. This being the case I found only some twenty pubs that deserved scrutiny and this would only make a book, nay booklet, of some forty pages. No good whatsoever, something had to be done.

I then spent six months studying every ghost in rural Surrey whether it be associated with an inn or not. The outcome was a volume of some 250 pages. Nobody would put up with that much of my crap, back to the drawing board.

The result was a courageous forage into London, Surrey; anything north of Sutton and Croydon. An intrepid odyssey along the no stopping red routes of Coulsdon, Thornton Heath, Kenley, Purley etc. etc. Can anybody really tell me where Merton, Mitcham, Morden and Malden begin and end, I asked myself rhetorically. Anyway this area brought forth a dozen or so haunted pubs so I shall not knock it.

Following this sojourn I decided to have a couple of more in depth pilgrimages into the wilds of southern Surrey. Many of the villages remain unaltered: Lingfield; Bletchingly (my grand parents abode); Godstone (excepting the traffic); Friday Street; Coldharbour; Abinger and Shere, to name but a few, remain some of the prettiest villages in the country. It was hard work finding haunted pubs but I stoically kept on course and cause and finally traced over fifty with a story to tell. I hope you enjoy them.

ROGER LONG

HAUNTED INNS OF SURREY

RED LION	Bletchingly
THE GREYHOUND	Carshalton
THE GEORGE	Chertsey
THE KINGS HEAD	Chertsey
THE CROWN	Chidingfold
PERCY ARMS	Chilworth
SILENT POND	Nr Chilworth
THE TARTAR (Deceased)	Cobham
RED LION	Coulsden
THE HARE AND HOUNDS	Croydon
BAR LATINO	Croydon
GEORGE INN (now deceased)	Croydon
WHITE HORSE	Dorking
THE BARLEY MOW	Englefield Green
HILLSIDE	London Road Egham
THE MARQUIS OF GRANBY	Scilly Isles roundabout, Esher
CLAREMONT HOUSE	Esher
WILLIAM IV	
(now Firkin something or other)	Ewell
NONSUCH PARK	Ewell
FARNHAM	
THE BUSH	Farnham
THE HOP BAG (now deceased)	Farnham
THE LION AND LAMB (now deceased)	Farnham
ASH MANOR	Ash Green, Nr Farnham
BOURNE MILL	Farnham
THE STEPHEAN LANGTON INN	Friday Street
THE WHITE HART	Frimley
THE KINGS ARMS & ROYAL HOTEL	Godalming
THE ANGEL	Guildford
YORK ROAD CAR PARK	Guildford
MERROW	Nr Guildford
CLANDON PARK	Guildford
KINGS ARMS	Hampton
HAMPTON VILLAGE	
THE HOLLY & LAUREL?	
BOTTLE & GLASS?	Holmwood
THE ROSE AND CROWN	Kenley
THE GREYHOUND INN	Lingfield

PUTTENDON MANOR	Lingfield
THE CROWN	Old Oxted
ROYAL OAK	Purley
THE ROEBUCK	Richmond Hill, Richmond
THE HOLE IN THE WALL	Richmond
THE TALBOT INN	Ripley
CASTLE RESTAURANT HOTEL	
(now CAFÉ ROUGE)	Sunbury
ROSSAL HOUSE	Sunbury
CRICKETERS (now FIELDER & FIRKIN)	Sutton
CARSHALTON HOUSE	Sutton
THE WHEATSHEAF	Thornton Heath
THE DONKEY	Tilford
THE GOLDEN GROVE	St. Anne's Hill, Twynersh
THE WHEATSHEAF	Virginia Water
BROOKLANDS	Weybridge
THE GROTTO	Weybridge
THE SHIP	Weybridge
GRANTLEY ARMS	Wonersh

RED LION
BLETCHINGLY

Lovely old village this, my maternal grandmother was born here in 1879 but I have never quite been able to find the address. There are some beautiful old buildings around the church and the church itself has a hermits cell probably the abode of Roger the Hermit who lived here in the 13TH century.

Bletchingly was known as the 'Rotten Borough', which I believe, is no reflection on the people but as with London's Rotten Rolnes an adaptation of the French 'Route du Roi' or Royal Route. As Henry VIII spent much of his time in the vicinity let us speculate that 'Rotten Borough' is a corruption of Royal Borough.

There are at least four very ancient inns in Bletchingly. No doubt my old granddad used them all. Two of the four were here in the 14TH century, The Red Lion (1309) and the Whyte Harte (1388). The other two followed not many years later. As yet the vast combines have not moved in, thank God, every pub still has its individual character.

The Red Lion stands midway up Castle Hill on the old A25 and is a picturesque pub both externally and internally. It was initially called The Maid and it is possible that the original maid (as in maiden) was an inhabitant of the now derelict and demolished castle.

It is a lady or maiden in grey that haunts the old inn. There is no record of any poor woman meeting an untimely end in the vicinity, but then, in the 14TH century very few people met a natural demise. So we don't know who she was but we know she's still about. In the absence of mine hosts I questioned the barmaid.

"I haven't seen or heard her," she replied, "But others working here have. Apparently it goes cold and you hear her footsteps on the passageway above." She shook her shoulders, "Its spooky, very spooky," she added.

THE GREYHOUND
CARSHALTON

What a lovely spot this is with its ponds, lawns and memorials. Pity about the traffic. In the good old days I used to drag a girt lorry around here, more scared that some icy patch would put me in the ponds rather than admiring them.

The exterior of The Greyhound suits the idyllic setting, this Surrey gem set in the London sprawl. It was built in the 1700's when anything Dutch was the vogue due to the amalgamation of the Royal families. This fashion is supported by the Dutch style gables of the inn. Legend dictates that there was a cockpit at The Greyhound but there is no evidence of it today. It is probably true but of very little historic interest. In the 1800's cockpits were nearly as common as dartboards are today.

On entering The Greyhound one realises that if Carlshalton is a village in London, internally it is a London pub in a village. It is vast with three or four bars all served from one central position. I like the place, there is always a picture to look at that you haven't noticed before, choose from the many and varying prints on the walls.

At my last visit there was some local concern about an anonymous man who had placed a statue on the green opposite in protest. Local 'teenagers' had pulled it down but the man had written to the local newspaper to say he was going to resurrect it.

This conversation piece gave me the opportunity to ask the landlady about her resident ghost. She was very busy and replied that she had not seen him but several of her staff had reported 'queer things'. Reputedly The Greyhound ghost is that of a traveller who was found frozen to death one winter's night. He lay on the doorstep wrapped in a cloak that obviously wasn't sufficient protection against the weather. Apparently his ghost has been witnessed both inside and outside the inn.

Before leaving I had a word with a gentleman I took to be mine host. Only the guvner sweeps up leaves in the car park.

"Spirits," he said, "Only ones I've seen come out of optics."

With that observation I left The Greyhound.

THE GEORGE
CHERTSEY

The George is one of my favourites and I use it whenever I drop into Chertsey. My visits however are now far fewer since the M25 (Europe's largest car park) came into being.

The George is another good setting for ghosts, it is ancient and possesses, rumour dictates, at least two priest holes and one secret passage. The building began life as a 14TH century hunting lodge before becoming a fully-fledged inn some 100 years later.

The spirit at The George is said to be that of yet another grey lady. This one is seldom seen but often heard walking between the upstairs bedrooms. Swift investigators rushing up the stairway have yet to catch a glimpse of her.

This invisible grey lady is unique among spirits in one respect, she has bulk. The landlady when being interviewed many years ago described how she had seen the centres of several beds show a deep indentation, as if somebody was sitting there. These strange occurrences were always accompanied by a sharp drop in temperature.

A story I heard from one of the locals some time ago, but as yet has no confirmation, is that a lady guest left in the middle of the night because somebody unseen was sitting on her chest, making it difficult to breathe.

I know the feeling. My massively overweight tabby has a similar habit.

THE KINGS HEAD
CHERTSEY

Mercifully parts of the old town and its pubs have been left intact. There may be a great gap in the middle and a one-way and no entry system that would fox a modern day Einstein but it is still possible to walk from one old part of the town to another. So I walked from The George to The Kings Head, another one time favourite of mine. Little has changed in this enchanting old pub, but there are too many portraits of scarlet robed judges for my peace of mind.

The Kings Head has a spectral monk. This one is reputed to rip the bedclothes off live-in barmaids. One poor Australian barmaid took flight one night and could not be encouraged back to pick up her belongings. Another barmaid also fled after seeing the spectral monk in another bedroom. There is reputed to be a blocked up passage here and a priest's hole. Could this priest be wandering out of his hole for sustenance, and other thwarted gratifications of the body I wonder?

I questioned the young man behind the bar. He had not heard of the tunnel or the priest's hole. He had however seen the spectral monk on several occasions and had felt his presence on several more. "You can tell when he is in a room and when he isn't," he stated.

Just then an older gentleman entered from upstairs. "Gentleman's asking about the ghost," the young man said.

"Oh," came the reply. "I've seen him often enough and smelt him. He stinks to high heaven."

Very unusual that, a ghost that smells. I've got a morbid outlook on life but the priest's hole cannot be found, what if the priest is still in there? And the spectre is trying to tell us so. After hundreds of years he'd stink a bit wouldn't he. It doesn't bare thinking about.

There are various other ghosts in Chertsey that I have heard of from numerous sources. The following two are dealt with at some length in Andrew Green's *Our Haunted Kingdom* (the ghost hunters bible).

The Cedars museum in Windsor Street was once a private dwelling. A doctor lived there in the 70's and regularly heard the patter of tiny feet from an upstairs bedroom. Even stranger was that the child's footsteps sounded as though they were traversing a hard surface like floorboards or lino. All the upstairs rooms had been thickly carpeted for decades.

An offset printers in Charles Street once had a spook named Henry who committed mild poltergeist activity. Henry was also fond of the old firm that he had probably worked for. As Henry made the previous firms letterheads appear on documents photographed by the new owners.

I noticed recently in Chertsey such names as Curfew Bell Road and the Curfew Garage. It reminded me of the old towns legendry story, the authenticity of which I am not at all certain. During the War of the Roses, the Duke of Warwick's nephew was captured by Yorkists and imprisoned in Chertsey. He was condemned to die at the sound of Curfew. Blanche Heriot, the condemned man's lover had applied for a reprieve to save him. Time was of the essence and plucky Blanche nearly met her death by swinging back and forth on the bell clanger thereby making sure that the curfew was not heard. Conveniently the old bell ringer was deaf and did not realise that something was amiss. A messenger rode poste haste with the reprieve and placed it at the Sergeant at Arms feet. The lover was pardoned and Blanche, bloodied, battered but deliriously happy, lived with him happily ever after.

The story crossed the Atlantic where it was transformed into a very bad and sickly romantic poem. The War of the Roses was changed to the English Civil War of Cromwell's time. Blanche became Bessie and the poetess then changed the Duke of Warwick's young nephews name to Basil Underwood. It was so bad that it just had to be a hit in the USA. Here's a line or two:

> Still the maiden clung more firmly
> And with trembling lips so white
> Said to hush her hearts wild throbbing
> Curfew shall not ring tonight

Late the proper comedians took over and changed the story to a crude song. Blanche who had become Bessie now metamorphosed into Nellie. I can remember very little of it, thank God, but a couple of lines went:

> Hang on the bell, Nellie, hang on the bell
> Your lover is locked in a cold prison cell
> As she swings to the left and swings to the right
> Remember, curfew must not ring tonight

The song was even worse than the poem but at least it had the good grace not to take itself seriously. Think if Blanche / Bessie / Nellie had had the sense to tie a load of sacking around the clapper she would have saved herself a lot of discomfort. I admit the story line would have suffered a little.

By the way, two ghostly figures are seen to make their way towards St Peters church on a specific night of the year. An old unco-operative sexton is being pleaded to by a young girl.

It's about as likely as the original story anyway.

THE CROWN
CHIDINGFOLD

The village of Chidingfold is as old as human time itself. The Romans found it conducive with glass making. The thorn on the village green was documented some 500 years ago and some nearby houses pre-date even that. My last, nay latest, visit to The Crown was in mid-October 2001. The villagers were preparing for their massive annual bonfire, fuel was piled high and there were signs saying 'NO MORE PLEASE'. Brenda Allaway, who takes a lot of my photographs, is a Surrey lass and informs me that the villagers used to take it in turns to stay in a caravan and act as night watchmen. Obviously to stop some killjoy from setting fire to it too early.

The Crown is 13TH century and was a stopping off place for the boy king Edward VI on his way to Shillinglee. It's original intent was as a resting place for Cistercian monks on their way from Winchester to Canterbury. Sustenance was provided from nearby Waverley Abbey. The original deeds still hang in The Crown's inglenook showing when the good brothers handed it over as an inn. It was let to a brewer named Thomas Godfare.

If ever a place should be haunted it is The Crown. It is the epitome of a grand old English inn. One would have thought that it would have a plethora of ghosts. When I enquired 15 years ago regulars told me that it had more ghosts than you could shake a stick at; nuns, monks, smugglers etc. etc.

Management, however, deny there are any. This time I tentatively enquired of three or four barmaids. They knew nothing, or were saying nothing. Consecutive landlords have put strange noises down to shrinking wood and other natural phenomena. (If of course that is not a contradiction in terms).

PERCY ARMS
CHILWORTH

Chilworth is a hamlet once famous for it's church and gunpowder mills. The church, the lofty St. Martha's, is still around, the gunpowder mills thankfully are not.

St. Martha's stands on ground where heathens once worshipped and where Christian martyrs were probably massacred. To the south of the strangely shaped church are five circular banks about one hundred feet in diameter, these are thought to have once held plinths for Bronze Age statues. There is definitely an atmosphere here.

But enough of this strange area and down to the Percy Arms. As it's name suggests it was once owned by the Duke of Northumberland, hence the name Percy. The Duke also owned the gunpowder mills that provided a livelihood for most of the neighbourhood and an untimely death for a few. Small accidents were a regular occurrence and more serious ones seemed to arrive in a sequence of about one every three years. In 1901 a great explosion caused the death of six local men, five of whom were literally blown to pieces. The sixth, 45 year old George Smithers, was blown 100 yards but although grievously wounded did not die instantly. He was carried back to the Percy Arms where he died in agony some two hours later. His autopsy, as with the other men, was held at the inn several days later.

It is thought to be George Smithers that set off the poltergeist activity in 1951. The poltergeist was in no way shy. He was quite happy to perform in crowded bars. Tankards and stools levitated in front of scores of customers and glasses of beer literally flew from counters. The then time landlady felt as if she was being pushed in the back on many occasions. Shutters rattled so violently on windless nights it convinced staff they were being burgled. The turnover of live-in staff was numerous. As with most poltergeist activity it ceased as suddenly as it had started.

What was the cause? Poor George Smithers has been blamed, admittedly he was the only one to die at the pub but the fragmented pieces of his colleagues were straightaways brought there for the inquest.

The Percy Arms has greatly altered since those days. It is now much upgraded and extended. It has an attractive restaurant and a very varied menu. Poor George Smithers 'the poltergeist' would hardly find the situation conducive with his antics.

Just before closing a thought has just struck me. Why did poor George Smithers wait exactly 50 years before performing? He died in 1901 and the poltergeist activity did not start until 1951. I just wonder if he reappears every 50 years. That means he is due to surface again in 2001. Oh dear, oh dear!!!!!

Whilst in the Chilworth area why not take a trip down to the Silent Pool.

SILENT POND
Between ALBURY and SHERE, Nr. CHILWORTH

What an incredibly beautiful and romantic part of the country this is. Park at Newlands Corner, have a pint in one of Shere's ancient inns, struggle to the top of Leith Hill, through to the water cress beds to Abinger Hammer where the little wooden man strikes the hour and then take in the beauty of the Silent Pool. There is hardly a ripple and the water is so clear you can see the bottom. Catch the pool in moonlight, pull out your sleeping bag and slumber as I did forty years ago on the first step of my hitch-hiking tour of the continent.
With apologies to our Omar: -

> Here with a loaf of bread beneath the bough
> A flask of wine, a book of verse – and thou

I wonder what did happen to Kathy; Europe was far too mundane for such as she. She worked her way (some say on her back) to Australia. Oh well,

> The moving finger writes and having writ moves on

Enough of this nostalgia let us look at the legend of the Silent Pool. Pantomime time.
Once in the early part of the 13TH century a cottage stood here. It was the abode of a woodman, his sturdy son and his beautiful daughter. One day a knight went by (no pun) and was pleased to dine with the humble woodman. As was her want the woodman's daughter took a nude bathe each day in the Silent Pool. The knight having depleted the woodman's humble vitals bestraddled his horse and rode on his way. In all probability this knight had noticed the young lady's absence from her father's cottage and was bent on a little deflowering. On hearing the knight's approach the maiden made for the shore to recover her clothes. Too late! The horseman had spurred his horse to the lakeside and encouraged the beast to trample her clothes. The knight tried to bribe and threaten the maiden to come out.

8

She refused and blushing with newfound modesty went deeper and deeper into the pool. Now being out of her depth and a poor swimmer she floundered and screamed for help. The sturdy brother ran to his sister's aid, but, being no better a swimmer than she, he clasped her in his arms and they both perished at the bottom of the Silent Pool. Sir knight, searching for more lively entertainment rode callously away. Here the story should have ended, but as the unfortunate woodman and his colleagues dragged the bodies from their watery graves they noticed a large white plume caught in a tree. The woodman immediately recognised it as coming from the knight's helmet and concluded that his children had been murdered. After many inquiries the woodman discovered that the knight in question was none other than Bad King John, regent of Britain, whilst his brother Richard was out crusading. He quickly sort out one of John's powerful enemies who in turn arranged an audience at Guildford Cathedral. The woodman attended the audience in disguise and retold his story. King John, who had evidently forgotten such a trifling incident, swore to have the murderer punished. The woodman pulled the feather from under his coat and openly accused him. The outcome of this outburst is unknown. But it is reputed to have been the event that initiated the unification of the barons that finally led to the sealing of the Magna Carta at Runnymede in 1215.

Honour was satisfied but apparently the ghost of the lovely maiden is not. In the evening of the appropriate time of year she makes her way down to the waters edge, disrobes and enters the Silent Pool. All is peaceful and serene until hoofbeats are heard and then there is a terrifying screaming and thrashing as the woodman's daughter once again sinks into her watery doom.

THE TARTAR (Deceased)
A3, COBHAM

I was not going to mention any stories from any towns or villages in this book unless they were connected with a pub. Cobham is, very tenuously, connected to an extinct pub. Had I gone into every strange happening and ghost story I have on file concerning Surrey it would have been an unsellable 250 pages.

There are Christmas night stories usually told by Uncle Ned with a large scotch or Aunt Mildred on her third schooner. There are half a dozen standard themes. Dead sons abroad contacting their loving mothers by phone. Ghosts rising from the grave and pointing at their murderers, old soldiers dropping dead as their forsaken lovers appear behind them in mirrors. Pictures dropping off walls at the instant their likeness perishes miles away and, worst of all, the vanishing hitch-hiker.

I had heard this story before but a far fully account appears in John Janaways *Haunted Surrey*. I have every respect for Mr Janaway and I am sure his attitude is as tongue in cheek as my own. On a wet and miserable night in 1947 a van driver was heading up the A3 near Cobham. Peering through his windscreen at the unrelenting rain the driver noticed a young girl attired only in a light dress, hitch-hiking. Considering the inclement conditions the driver broke his rules and stopped for her. After several attempts at conversation that were not reciprocated the driver began to be irritated. His passenger would not say a word. Apparently, through some sort of sign language she indicated that he turn into Cobham village. This he proceeded to do. The van traversed High Street and turned into Church Street. Here the drenched young lady indicated that she wished to alight. The driver could see the house up a short drive and being a knight of the road suggested that she take his overcoat to put over her head, adding that he would collect it in a week's time. The speechless young lady gratefully accepted his offer.

Guess what?

A week or so later the van driver called at the door and was greeted by a middle-aged man. The driver explained about the hitch-hiker and his overcoat. The strained man solemnly pointed out that the young girl concerned was his daughter and that she had died ten years previously. She had been to a dance at the Tartar Inn, had hitch-hiked home and gone to bed. She had fallen asleep reading and the candle had set fire to her bedclothes. The father informed the van driver that he was not the first one to undergo this experience and then insisted that he take him to a nearby graveyard where his daughter lay buried.

You've guessed it.

There on the gravestone lay the drivers overcoat.

It gets better.

On his way home the driver felt a touch on his arm and the noise of the engine seemed to say "Thank You."

I have heard similar stories the length and breadth of Britain and Europe. The USA has a thousand plus.

Now I have brought Cobham into this book here's one or two other stories about the village.

Painshill Park with its beautiful lake fed from the Mole is the centrepiece of Cobham. It has many follies that have recently been renovated by the local authorities. One of these follies is a tall redbrick prospect tower that overlooks the A3. I have always found this tower a little disconcerting but more of that later.

It is a smaller house once owned by a famous actress that would seem unfriendly to its occupants. If Quenhells decides it doesn't like you it lets you know it. This actress found that she could only spend a few minutes in the kitchen without being forced to get out by an overpowering atmosphere. The lavatory had the same effect on both family and friends. So here we have a building that exudes a malevolent hostility. Don't knock it until you've experienced it. It aint funny.

Field Marshal, Jean Louis, Lord Ligonier haunts the A3 near Painshill Park. Once again within a stones throw of the prospect tower. Not that there should be anything daunting about a folly, after all, nobody good or evil has ever lived there. Ligonier was a large man, a French Huguenot, who fled to England in the1750's to escape religious persecution. He soon became an officer in the British army and fought at Malplaquet, sustaining over a score of bullet wounds. Eventually Ligonier became Commander-in-Chief of British forces and retired to Cobham Place. There he died in 1770 but apparently his spirit could not rest. He has been seen many times on the Portsmouth Road. The spirit, which is luminous, is dressed in an army great coat. It is a scary spectre because on closer scrutiny it is noticed that the Field Marshal has empty eye sockets.

Could it have been the grotesque Ligonier that caused an internationally known pop group to veer off the A3 in the 60's? They described seeing a terrifying monster of a man. No doubt they had experienced a 'bad trip'.

Can you imagine such headlines as 'The phantom marksman of hellfire pass' being applied to the Surrey stockbroker belt? Possibly not, but they certainly were in the early 50's. Car after car had their windscreens holed by what was thought to be bullets. Any hour of the day or night terrified motorists heard a bang followed by a cracked windscreen. One motorist had a 'bullet' go through his side door. He called the police, who in turn took the car to pieces. No bullet was found but the hole was real enough. In fact in all the attacks (over 40) no bullet was ever found.

So what was causing the holes in the windscreens and side doors? And where were they coming from?

Stones thrown up from your tyres? Too regular, thrown up stones would not usually hit windscreens. A catapult shooting ball bearings? Possible but it would take a fair old catapult to put a projectile through a steel door. An air rifle? Too inept to do the damage. Possibly an alien with a ray gun. I jest not. It really was put forward as an idea from the lunatic fringe.

The ghost at Claremont House that bordered the route making projectiles elevate and explode? I don't really think so. Be that as it may, the police found it impossible to trace the culprit. They employed a roving police car that picked up complaints. Rushing to the scene they let loose bloodhounds, but to no avail. A break of sorts came when an anonymous letter arrived in a schoolboys writing. It claimed to be from the 'phantom marksman'. Unfortunately it did not explain how a bullet could penetrate a windscreen and disappear. However, the letter did state that the culprit was moving away and that the attacks would cease. They did not cease, if anything they intensified. After nearly two years the attacks became more infrequent and finally terminated. There is still no satisfactory explanation.

Generations of bell ringers at the village here have reported sightings of a spectral blue donkey. I really have no further comment.

Or perhaps I do…………..

There is an old lawyers trick called the Blue Donkey Syndrome. It is where a solicitor / QC will say "Take no notice whatsoever of this statement," knowing fully well that you will then be unable to forget it. Hence, I do not want you to imagine a blue donkey – I bet that is just what you did do.

RED LION
COULSDEN

A large and busy old pub this, right where the traffic squeezes to a halt on the Brighton Road. I am told that the Red Lion was rebuilt in 1928 on the site of a far smaller pub. When I was first here in the 1970's there were three distinct bars. When I returned in 2001 they seemed to have altered into one vast front bar.

In the 1800's a nearby (2 miles) farmhouse was proving difficult to sell. The reason being that ghostly horses hooves were heard outside at 2 am. Apparently they have remained ever since. Similar hoof beats have been heard outside the Red Lion. The story is that a well-known farmer who dwelt at the farm regularly made for the inn at post haste. One night he lost control of the beast as he sped down the long steep hill (A3) and was thrown outside the Red Lion, cracking his pate. He died shortly after. The horse panicked and galloped back to the farmhouse.

Personally I should be very surprised if one could hear anything outside the Red Lion any hour of the twenty-four. And, if the farmer charged down the hill at top speed he was the last person to do so. The several hundred yards from hilltop to Red Lion can take up to 15 minutes on a busy day.

Frances D Stewart has several poltergeist tales to relate about Coulsdon. But as I have neither visited nor investigated these accounts I do not feel qualified to comment upon them.

THE HARE AND HOUNDS
CROYDON

This beautiful old pub old pub with its wrought iron balcony looks out of place on Croydon's Purley Way. The building dates back to 1773 when initially it was a farmhouse. It metamorphosed into a licensed house in 1816. The Hare and Hounds geographical position making it an ideal spot for the changing of horses. The London to Brighton stage route, England's busiest, passed by the front door.

In 1805 a group of people went in search of a man-monster who attacked every woman he met. Although tall and rather stout he had been reported to leap over palings and hedgerows some 12 feet high or more. Such events the locals decided could only be achieved by a spirit and not a man. How one can be physically attacked by a spirit I cannot imagine. There have however been cases where finger marks have been left on the limbs of people that have supposedly been gripped by ghosts. On hearing this story I looked up my file on Spring Heeled Jack, but there were no sightings of that gentleman prior to 1830. Some twenty years after the Croydon monster. Also Jack was of athletic build, not at all stout.

Nothing supernatural has been seen outside the Hare and Hounds for many years. No self respecting ghost would come anywhere near the hurley burley of the Purley Way. Still the Hare and Hounds maintains a cordial welcome. It is worth a visit just for that.

BAR LATINO
CROYDON

I am a little reluctant to describe the goings on at the King Cellars (now Bar Latino) at Croydon in the late 70's and 80's. It was a lengthy series of poltergeist activities that evoked the interest of at least half a dozen of this country's most famous ghost hunters.

The King's Cellars at Park Street in Croydon were built on the site of a far older building. It was rumoured that many bones were found when the footings were dug and also that a young girl had once committed suicide in an adjacent building. Things immediately began to happen. Glasses filled themselves, as did drip trays. The spectre of a young girl appeared regularly and was heard to whisper, "Help me." Strange things happened on a regular basis and in one month in 1979, a quiche and its plate rose 6 inches off of a table and remained in mid-air for several seconds. A candle complete with bottle flew 6 feet from a shelf, other candles burnt down very rapidly, two brandy glasses did a somersault and a friendly dog would not go near its favourite corner. Incidentally in a corner where low laughter had been heard an unusual electric fire occurred that could not be explained by fire investigators. In 1980 the tills adopted a life of their own, ringing up the most ridiculous amounts and causing suspicion to be cast on the most honest of staff. Such events brought media interest and a programme on the Kings Cellars was televised. Unfortunately the poor investigator was met with such a pungent aroma that he nearly 'gave up the ghost' if you'll pardon the pun.

I have no record of the hauntings ceasing and must look further into this case. I know that the pub has been altered and renamed and assume that the spooks have gone away. They usually do – given time.

I should like to thank Guy Lyon Playfair for firstly interesting me in the case. His report appears in his *Haunted Pub Guide*.

GEORGE INN (now deceased)
CROYDON

It is a great pity that the old George Inn at Croydon is no longer. There is a massive George Inn there now, a Wetherspoon outlet, one of our better modern conglomerations. I am told, probably reliably, that the original George was further down George Street and became a bank. If this is so perhaps it will reincarnate as a trendy wine bar.

Many years ago, nobody knows how many, a wicked old landlady at the George murdered her lodgers and then boiled their remains in a cauldron. For what reason I am not quite sure. It may have made the bodies more flexible and therefore easier to secrete, or, God forbid, they were served up as some sort of nutritious delicacy. It has been done before, you know.

It is said that the landlady acquired the nickname of Old Mother Hotwater and that the spirits of her luckless lodgers frequented the building for many years.

It would be a pity to leave Croydon without a look around other venues.

There was a very interesting murder case here in 1907. A certain man named Brinkley had forged a will in his own favour getting his friend an accountant to witness it, stating that it was part of a Masonic invitation he needed witnessing. After inheriting the money much to the chagrin of the deceased's daughter, who had started proceedings against him, Brinkley decided his duped accountant friend might cause him trouble. He called on the accountant at his lodgings with a bottle of oatmeal stout. They both enjoyed a glass. Brinkley asked if he might have a glass of water and was left in the room. Several minutes after consuming the water he took his leave. Shortly afterwards the accountant also went out. Mr and Mrs Beck, with whom the accountant lodged, entered the room. Seeing the bottle of stout and thinking waste not want not, they both imbibed. Within several hours both were dead; however not the intended victims. Brinkley was apprehended, tried, convicted and hanged at Wandsworth Prison on August 13TH 1907.

I don't know why I mention this; it's got nothing to do with ghosts.

A tempestuous pilot in a RAF World War II leather flying jacket appeared to the owner of a Croydon house in the late 70's. Coincidentally the young owner was a collector of Second World War memorabilia. It was a tailors dummy dressed in SS uniform that seemed to upset the pilot as he strode about the house complete with helmet and oxygen mask. After several appearances the pilot disappeared, but his invisible being was still at large. It gave vent to his animosity by hurling the tailor's dummy, complete with uniform, the length of the hall. A few nights later the spirit made himself known by pulling the bedclothes off of a female guest in the spareroom. This was beyond the pale; the owners called in a local priest for an attempt to exorcise the unwanted spirit.

Playful to the end, at the exorcism ceremony, the owner's wife felt her bra strap being plucked although she was standing alone. All that can be stated about the origin of this case is that a physic investigator found that the house was built on the site of the old Croydon airport.

Well good luck to you mate. You might have been one of the few that saved us in the Battle of Britain. What's a little blanket tugging and bra snapping between friends? As our young pilots use to say "You are only truly alive when living close to death."

Frances D Stewart mentions a plethora of ghosts at Croydon's North End. In her book *Surrey Ghosts Old and New* she mentions a Victorian lady, pale and beautiful, who promptly disappears. Also a nun and a working class man complete with rolled up sleeves a collarless shirt and a boiler suit.

WHITE HORSE
DORKING

Dorking is an ancient and prosperous little town surrounded on all sides by some of the most attractive countryside in England. In ancient times this was the junction of Roman Stane Street and the trade route later known as the Pilgrims Way.

Its close proximity to the junction may have resulted in the 15TH century White Horse being called the Cross House until 1780. There is however a school of thought that believes that the cross was the symbol of the inns one time owners the Knights of St John of Jerusalem. In those days, the mid 13TH century, there would have been a completely different building here, some type of basic hostel.

Dickens slept at the White Horse and used its description in Pickwick Papers. It has no doubt had countless other famous guests over the centuries. Its ghost is said to be royalty, the ninth Earl of Norfolk no less. The Earl lived just down the road in glorious Deepdene House. This jovial spirit, who may be slightly in his cups, is said to parade through the bar complete with robes of state and ducal crown. He is thought to be lost on the way to Deepdene but I find this a little hard to believe.

I revisited the White Horse one Monday lunchtime. I do not drink on a Monday or Tuesday so I settled down to soup and a roll. I made tentative enquiries about the ghostly Earl to several bar staff, a waiter and a seemingly very efficient receptionist. I was greeted by staring blank faces on each occasion. Reconnoitring the bars for obvious locals and seeing none I called it a day.

Talking of Deepdene this majestic house once owned by the Duke of Norfolk was, in it's hayday, frequently visited by Disraeli. Here he wrote much of his novel Coningsby. Amongst notable others John Aubrey, the antiquary, stayed at Deepdene. Later a gentleman named Thomas Hope lived at Deepdene. He built a mausoleum and scattered the ashes of his 8 year old son. The mausoleum was never a settled place. Various owners of the vast estate have built follies and a network of tunnels. Was it from one of these disused subterranean passages that a tall spiritual figure with an antelope type head appeared in the 1950's? It was sufficiently realistic to scare the life out of several witnesses before disappearing. This smacks of black magic to yours truly.

On the same subject there have been reports of a black headless horseman near Dorking church. The hooves are silent and traverse Chart Lane, Pixham Lane and Punchbowl Lane area.

Frances D Stewart in her book *Surrey Hauntings Old and New*, tells of an antique shop that was once The Queens Arms Inn. The writer interviewed the owner in the early 1990's and discovered a history that went back to 1428. Apparently the property belonged to William Mullins a wealthy cordwainer (shoemaker / leather worker) who sailed on the Mayflower.
In her interview Stewart heard of stock moving and pictures revolving. There would seem to be two ghosts here. One is a young girl in a grey skirt and the other a small lady, also in grey, who sits weeping. Could one be mourning the loss of the other I wonder?

THE BARLEY MOW
ENGLEFIELD GREEN

This is a fine epitome of all that's good in an English inn. The licence goes back some 350 years but the building is much older. It was run for some time by a friend of mine and I have spent many pleasant evenings gazing across the village green at some local cricket match. My friend the landlord always swore the place was haunted by a dying Frenchman. He had a rough outline of the story, which I have since researched.
The story concerns the last fatal duel fought in England and this involved six Frenchmen. Two duellists and their seconds. The scene was just a stones throw away at Priest Hill. A local field was known as Barthelemy's Field after the victor. However, Berthelemy was later hanged at Tyburn for a double murder. The incident happened in October 1852. A local doctor was approached by three Frenchmen who asked the way to Windsor. He later came across a fourth Frenchman who directed him to where a friend had had a shooting accident. Finding a man dying from a gunshot wound in his friend's arms the doctor directed locals to take the poor man on a hurdle to the Barley Mow. There he endured a slow and painful death. Four of the Frenchmen were detained later that day. One at the scene and three at Waterloo, a fifth man had completely disappeared. The four were later charged with the murder of Monsieur Gournet, the unfortunate victim of the duel. The accused were found not guilty of murder but guilty of manslaughter. Barthelemy and his three colleagues were sentenced to two months imprisonment. The judge bore in mind that they had all been incarcerated for the previous five months. He must have been a little

perplexed as the duel created a precedent in England. Gournet, the victim, was a popular man and en masse his countrymen turned up to carry his coffin from the Barley Mow to Egham church, a distance of some 1½ miles. The pallbearers changed three times.

It is the gurgling death throws of Monsieur Gournet that are still heard coming from a bedroom at the Barley Mow.

Just down the hill towards Egham once stood a house that caused much controversy.

THE RED LION, BELTCHINGLY
Home of another lady in grey. Also footsteps are heard and it is spooky, very spooky

THE GREYHOUND, CARSHALTON
Haunted by a traveller found frozen to death on the inn's doorstep

THE GEORGE, CHERTSEY
This has one of the country's many 'grey ladies'

THE KINGS HEAD, CHERTSEY
Home of a rather nasty spectral monk

THE CROWN, CHIDINGFOLD
Strange noises over the years have been put down to shrinking wood

THE PERCY ARMS, CHILWORTH
Poltergeist activity in the 50's and 60s was reputedly caused by a local worker
who was injured in a gunpowder explosion and later died at the inn

THE RED LION, COULSDON

Outside this inn a spooked horse threw its rider, fatally. The panicking horse's
hooves may still be heard

THE HARE AND HOUNDS, CROYDON

In 1805 the regulars formed a posse to find the ghostly monster who was
attacking their womenfolk

BAR LATINO, CROYDON

Once the Kings Cellars, this had such ferocious poltergeist activity that no bar staff would remain

THE WHITE HORSE, DORKING

Mentioned by Dickens. Here, a regal ghost (the ninth Earl of Norfolk) often mistakes the inn for his nearby house

THE BARLEY MOW, ENGLEFIELD GREEN
Haunted by a French duellist who died here

WILLIAM IV
(now FIRKIN SOMETHING OR OTHER), EWELL
Roman coins were found here and a spectral coach and horses pass the door

HILLSIDE
LONDON ROAD, EGHAM

Have you ever wondered if a resident ghost would enhance or lower the price of your property? Well the case of a villa, Hillside at Egham, put the precedent to the test; three times in fact.

The owner Mr Charles Barret bought the property in 1890. He successfully let the large and pleasant building out to various tenants until 1903, when it was let to Mr Stephen Phillips. Phillips was a fairly well known writer and poet. Maybe it was the writer's artistic temperament that caused him to hear inexplicable noises that sounded like a child strangling to death. Phillips was so upset that he moved out of the house and into a nearby hotel forfeiting his £70 per annum rent, a not inconsiderable sum.

It later transpired that previous inexplicable actions had occurred; strange knocks, footfalls, doors opening etc. Still more worrying was that Phillips 4 year old daughter had seen a little old man creeping about the house. When Phillips enquired of the local community he was told that an old farmer had murdered a young female child on the original site, prior to the building of Hillside.

The high profile of the case brought it to the attention of the media. The Daily Express gave an account of it. The result of this being an action brought against the paper and Phillips. The owner stated that he had not been able to let the place since the article and charged the Express and Phillips with 'slander of title'. The affair was settled out of court, the owner receiving £200.

In 1906 the Daily Mail, obviously not learning from the Express's experience quoted Phillips story from a magazine called 'Light'. The owner who was still having difficulty letting the building sued both publications. The Mail and Light fought the case, their barrister suggesting that the house was unpopular, not through any haunted reputation but because it fronted the A30 London to Exeter road. He stated that above 30 cars passed each day and that the dust must be intolerable. Despite the barristers eloquence the case succeeded. The Daily Mail was instructed to pay £90 and Light £10.

However, some months later the Daily Mail made a successful appeal.

THE MARQUIS OF GRANBY
SCILLY ISLES ROUNDABOUT, ESHER

Years ago I was travelling back from a Surrey town with a friend. We had been to see an illegal bare knuckle fight but that is beside the point. My friend, a PhD and therefore not very bright, exclaimed "Look Rog! The Scilly Isles Roundabout, just like those off of the Cornish coast."

"No," says I, knowing that my being pedantic annoyed him. "They are the Isles of Scilly."

"Well, f****** know all," he replied, "Tell me who the Marquis of Granby was? His bald head adorns a thousand boards but nobody has a clue who he was."

Do you know, I didn't know, so I looked up this well celebrated if unknown figure - here goes.

John Manners (1721-1770) eldest son of the third Duke of Rutland, distinguished soldier. During the Battle of Warburg, as colonel of The Blues, he led an inspired and courageous cavalry charge. The story goes that it was a hot and windy day. During the charge his wig blew off exposing a shiny pate that acted as a guiding light for his troops. The Blues won the day and Manners action brought forth the saying "Going for it bald headed." Manners was an extremely brave and caring man. As his wounded and disabled non-commissioned officers were invalided out from the front line Manners bought pubs for them. Hence his popularity on inn signs and his dying in debt of some £37,000 (the equivalent today is roughly £3 million). A fine upstanding chap.

But let us return to the Marquis of Granby at Esher.

The pub is old, about 400 years old and has a commanding and austere aspect to it. It has had various extensions over the years and at one stage it swallowed a group of adjacent cottages. Dickens mentions the Granby in Pickwick Papers. Sam Weller, the boots and Pickwick's ally visit the inn where his mother dispenses hot pineapple rum.

A landlord in the 60's heard a sound like skirts rustling coming from an extensive and disused walk-in cupboard. My friend, mentioned above, and I spoke to the landlord at the time. He was a brave man because although he had endured a certain amount of ridicule from his regulars he would not be dissuaded from his account. The landlord did not enter the cupboard; he was about to do so when he noticed a Bible had been placed against the door. In his 25 years of residence he neither moved the Bible nor opened the cupboard door. Whilst in Esher one should visit the famous Claremont House.

CLAREMONT HOUSE
ESHER

On the outskirts of Esher stands the resplendent Claremont House. Claremont was constructed for Sir John Vanbrugh in 1708. He sold it on to the Duke of Newcastle who in turn sold it on to Clive of India. Rumour has it that Claremont was never in the same family for two generations.

Claremont has a placid man made lake only 50 yards from the A3. The lake is the site of a regular haunting. Near the grotto by the lake a man is seen. He wears gaiters and an old fashioned coat of dark brown. He is about fifty years of age and would appear to be a gamekeeper, or is he?

In 1714 Claremont's second owner, Thomas Holles-Pelham, Duke of Newcastle and Prime Minister engaged the famous landscape gardener William Kent to do some massive alterations to the estate. Kent altered waterways and created a beautiful lake fed by water from a grotto. He also constructed an island in the lake and a romantic bridge to span the two. The work took several years. When it came time for financial settlement the Duke offered only £100. A frightful scene followed. The upshot was that the Duke called for two burly henchmen to throw Kent into the lake he had created. A week later Kent was caught in the Claremont grounds with two loaded pistols. The Dukes 'bouncers' arrived and Kent was once again deposited in his own lake. The famous landscaper never recovered, he died a week later from an ague, possibly brought about by his two cold duckings.

Who is the mystery spirit that haunts the lakeside, could it be William Kent still waiting to be paid.

WILLIAM IV
(now Firkin something or other)
EWELL

The pretty village of Ewell seems to have been systematically spoilt. There are still unspoilt patches but they are few. Even the by-pass seems to have increased the traffic in the centre. I wonder what Holman Hunt, arguably Ewell's most famous resident, would have made of it. I wonder what he would think now if he left his dreaming stream and drifted with Rossetti and Milais up to the King Billy. It would take them the best part of twenty minutes to cross the High Street that's for sure. But more of Holman Hunt later firstly lets have a word about good old King Billy (the publicans king).

He was the third son of George III, known as the sailor king. His popularity on nearly 1000 boards is due to his personal interest in the 1830 beer act. King Billy helped its speedy passage through parliament. The bill, cutting the tax on ale gave rise to a song in the 1830's, its chorus being:

> So long we'll sing
> Live Billy the king
> Who bated the tax on beer

The old William IV building still stands in Ewell High Street but it is now part of the Firkin group. Excavations near the inn once turned up Roman coins and pottery, also the bones of various animals. This would seem to have very little to do with the spectral coach and horses that pass the inn's door. The coach is more often heard than seen. The creaking of wheels, the neighing of horses and the jingle of reins seem to be the ingredients in this rather weak haunting. A pub of this stature deserves a more colourful ghost. There are a number of other ghosts in Ewell.

NONSUCH PARK
EWELL

Nonsuch Palace is no more but the 300 acre park, where kings once walked is open to the public. The local populace interspersed with tourists and dogs stride its attractive paths.

Seldom seen walking the paths but fairly frequently observed by motorists passing the main gate is a spectral gentleman in a black cloak. The man stands for several seconds observing the pathway that once ran to the old palace building. Rumour has it that he is surreptitiously waiting for a Victorian woman who was two-timing her husband. The lover's vigil is in vain. The husband found out about his wife's indiscretions and did her to death. That's Victorians for you, no sense of humour.

Quite a vivid manifestation of the waiting lover appeared before two schoolmasters in the 1970's. They described the apparition as a tall, dark and gaunt man who disappeared after several seconds.

26 Ewell High Street, once an antique shop.

On my most recent visit to Ewell the above premises was now an embroidery centre. In probably the greatest book on ghosts *Our Haunted Kingdom*, Andrew Green visits number 26 when it was an antique shop coupled with a motor accessories business. The old building is reputed to have a blocked off underground tunnel that once connected with Nonsuch Palace. The demolished palace was built by Henry VIII and our Henry is the main suspect for the unaccountable footsteps that have been heard about the building. The main cause of concern seems to be where two staircases meet. The atmosphere here is said to be electrifying and it is here in the late 60's that a female tenant was rudely pushed by an unseen assailant.

There have been rumours of spectral ladies and gentlemen in 18TH century attire roaming the gardens of Bourne Hall in Spring Street. Expecting to find an ancient manor I was a little surprised to find a vast and modern building that seemed to cater for every human activity of mind and body. Not a good stamping ground for ghosts one would have thought. Still one never knows.

This is more like it. St Marys is an ancient church but newer than the 15TH century tower that stands like a mysterious sentinel. It is all that remains of the previous medieval church. Take a darkening evening and anyone who cannot feel the atmosphere here, to use modern phraseology, must be 'brain dead'. Here on twilight summer evenings the plague children once buried in vast numbers here come out to play. Look quickly to your left or right – what was that? – a trick of the light – probably. Or was it a swift and sylph like ragged urchin dodging between the gravestones playing hide and seek? There lives were short and full of misery so let us not begrudge them a little fun on the other side of he veil.

The previously mentioned painter Holman Hunt was returning to his home from the station one dark night when he was accosted by a massive and ferocious white creature. Just when it was about to attack him physically it disappeared. Seeing that we are a little far south for an extremely nimble polar bear we must assume he saw a ghost.

FARNHAM

For its size this is the most haunted town in England. This necessitates my being very brief, here goes.

First to the historic Farnham Castle. The gateway of the great Norman keep, built by Henry of Blois, King Stephens's brother, is haunted by a very scary blob.

A stern faced lady in a fawn gown and chord girdle has also been witnessed at the gatehouse.

Fox Tower is the home of the spirit of Bishop Morley who restored the castle for Charles II. The Bishop's ghost is a rarity, it is seen and heard. Morley is also held responsible for a peel of ghostly bells that is sometimes heard. Incidentally Bishop Morley slept in a coffin.

The Great Hall has the shade of a murmuring monk.

The stairs outside have often witnessed a phantom dancing girl. A figure in grey haunts another stairway, a second blob appears in a bedroom, ghostly footsteps are heard in passageways and yet more footsteps climb the external stairs.

Farnham church has a ghostly shadowy congregation with splendidly attired officials; burning incense is also detected. An old lady dressed in brown enters the church and disappears, an inexplicable mist obscures the vision of mortal worshippers and the champing of a horse is often heard outside. Also a white lady may appear at the top of the tower.

Moving on; the Rangers House in Farnham Park is reputedly haunted by a pretty young girl while Castle Street has a phantom coach from which a dandy alights. The Castle Theatre harboured the ghost of a local murderer and a phantom nanny dressed in old fashioned attire appears at a private house in East Street whenever a baby is about to be born.

Vernon Lodge that housed the library is haunted by a figure thought to be Charles I. The ill destined King was housed here en-route to London after his capture.

Peter Underwood (author of many great ghost books including *Ghosts and How To See Them*) takes a saunter down Farnhams West Street and informs us of: -

A shop with a spectral black dog, an old woman standing still and mournful in what is now a bathroom, a ghostly and unaccountable roll of drums, a jewellers shop revisited by its long dead founder and a mop capped little old lady who hobbles with incredible speed.

Incidentally an elegant young Edwardian couple stroll both East and West Street and there is a restaurant in West Street haunted by another graceful couple. This time the man is attired in Victorian guard's uniform. The town boasts a female apparition in the same building as a maltmaster (who drowned in a vat). Peter Underwood also tells us of a ghost train on a long since demolished railway track and I have often heard tell of a phantom Roman army marching towards the town and there is a Victorian lady who haunts a cottage in Waverley Lane.

Now to Waverley Abbey on the outskirts of Farnham. Atmospheric Waverley Abbey dates from the 12Th century and was the first Cistercian abbey to be built in England. This vast and beautiful building was destroyed by Thomas Cromwell after the abbot has beseeched him to save it. The reputation of the monks was unblemished but Waverley went the way of many others. What is left of the abbey has a romantic aura. Twas always so, Sir Walter Scott used it for his book Waverley. Ironically the writer originated the book whilst staying in Waverley Abbey House, built from the stones of the ruined abbey itself.

The ghost of Waverley Abbey is yet another monk. The unfortunate brother was hung, drawn and quartered during the reformation. Having ones guts pulled out whilst still living cannot be much fun and it possibly sentenced this poor monk to an earthbound existence. However, people who have witnessed this apparition say that the monk is earnestly and methodically seeking something.

I put it to you, with no evidence whatsoever, that this apparition is not the poor tortured brother who died for his faith but an entirely different entity. A brother who had hidden something valuable and has now returned to find it. We all know that greed has far more pulling power than faith. Search on brother.

THE BUSH
FARNHAM

The Bush Hotel is probably the only haunted inn in Farnham that hasn't been demolished or changed its status. An alehouse in the 13TH century it has remained constant to the licensed trade ever since. One bedroom at the Bush is haunted by an old style serving maid. Ancient as the hills this lady is meticulous to the point of being pedantic. She gives the impression of being busy to the extreme. However, her appearances are getting less frequent as she slides into semi-retirement. But she seems to feel needed on special occasions. The last time this apparition appeared it was in the room of a young lady who was getting married the following day.

Here are a couple of haunted establishments that once were pubs.

THE HOP BAG (now deceased)
FARNHAM

One would have thought that in an old town like Farnham, that is inundated with ghosts and pubs, that oft the twain would meet - apparently not. As always I have kept the haunted pubs separate from the other spectres. They are disappointingly few in number. Firstly there was the Hop Bag, situated near the centre of town this pub was an old coaching inn.

Guests at the Hop Bag were often awakened by the neighing of horses and a heavy coach clattering into the yard. The sound persisted after the days of the horse drawn vehicle were long over and even after the inn closed for business. There are some quite recent reports of this phenomenon it has a touch of the quite incomprehensible time-warp theory about it.

Another inn that is no longer is: -

THE LION AND LAMB (now deceased)
FARNHAM

The Lion and Lamb Courtyard, once a pub and restaurant is now an upmarket parade of shops. During its restaurant era it was regularly visited by the ghost of a genteel old lady. The phantom looked real indeed especially when she joined the queue to be seated. When questioned as to her seating preference she would disappear. At one time the old lady was said to be putting in a couple of appearances each day. Unfortunately she has moved on.

Another ghost, a young lady in Victorian clothes, was seen quite regularly outside the Lion and Lamb. She seemed to be waiting to use the town pump. Pump and well have long since gone, as has the spectral lady. In all probability driven out by modifications.

BOURNE MILL
FARNHAM

Bourne Mill was mentioned in the Doomsday Book. It is reckoned to be the longest continuous business in Farnham. The working part of the mill has gone and is now a centre that specialises in wooden gazebos, sheds, garden figures, garden furniture and much, much more.

In the years of Farnham castle being an active garrison firewood and gunpowder were stored at the mill. Quite a lethal combination one would have thought. As far as I know there were no serious accidents.

My association with Bourne Mill came about in the 1960's when it was used as a drinking club. I constructed many a hangover here. It was well known than that the premises had long been haunted by an attractive lady clad in a crinoline dress. Sweet and charming as the lady was (or is) she must have been tough enough to withstand the buildings many metamorphosis. Her wandering / floating ground was along a hallway next to the drinking club; just above what is now a small tea room. Genteel as the lady would seem to be she must have been unshocked by or insulated against the language that erupted from the club.

As I wandered around Bourne Mill in Autumn 2001, I was amazed by the number of garden statuettes that surround the small pond and many hidden pathways. There are literally thousands peaking out between sheds and gazebos. Whoever designs some of the gargoyles and ogres must have experienced quite a lot of psychological trauma. Some of the faces on the ugly figures are unbelievable malign. It would take a very strong minded man to stay the night (preferably a stormy one) in one of the gazebos surrounded by such company.

Whilst in this part of Farnham I was reminded of a horrendous haunting that happened in Ash Green, a stones throw away, the premises are private, please respect.

ASH MANOR
ASH GREEN, Nr. FARNHAM

Ash Manor at Ash Green originated in 1279 but obviously has been much altered over the centuries. It has the perfect pedigree for haunting. It was built on the site of a fortified monastery that in turn was thought to have been erected on the site of an ancient Druid temple. A businessman named

Kelly bought Ash Manor in 1935. He was not informed of its somewhat chequered reputation. It was not long before the Kelly family began to experience all sorts of knockings and tappings. The master bedroom received a series of distinct raps on the door at regular intervals. Kelly tried to catch or at least witness the perpetrator but it soon became obvious that this was no flesh and blood intruder. Feeling worried for the safety of his family the owner called upon the services of professional ghost layers.

The knocking became worse, the ghost layers coming up with a cock and bull story about a young farmer slaying his unfaithful lover on the premises. If such a thing had happened Kelly figured that the locals would remember it. Such events are seldom forgotten they are more likely to be embellished. No record could be found and Kelly dismissed his ghost layers as charlatans.

Hauntings at Ash Manor were increasing and becoming more vivid. Several visitors witnessed a dark man standing in the door of the oast house that was opposite the main building. Also family dogs were badly affected by the house.

One guest, a Mr Miller, followed the dark spectre one night with the intention of blasting him with a shotgun. The guest was surprised when his shotgun suddenly flew from his grip and his cap followed it at a distance of some yards. To add to the melee the sound of galloping unseen horses was heard in the grounds.

The most indelible ghost of Ash Manor was witnessed by the owner one night. It appeared in the bedroom and was visible for several minutes. Kelly described him as a very short and plump man attired in muddy breeches, green coat, slouch hat and a red and white spotted neckerchief. Thinking this interloper to be a burglar Kelly grabbed him by the arm only to find his fingers gripping fresh air.

The small figure was witnessed on several separate occasions, the most terrifying encounter being reserved for the lady of the house, Mrs Kelly. The little man was dressed as before but this time it was noticed that the aforementioned red and white neckerchief was actually a blood soaked bandage and that the poor spirits throat had been slashed from ear to ear.

In 1936 a flashlight camera was set up by investigators to cover several of the bleeding ghosts favourite spots. The result showed a couple of substantial blurs in the little mans special corner. Photography was less sophisticated in those days but experts agreed that no tampering had taken place.

Like most ghost stories there is no ending. Who was the little man? Was he murdered by the dark man near the oast house? Did he commit suicide? We shall never know.

THE STEPHEN LANGTON INN
FRIDAY STREET

Built in 1930 on the site of a previous pub, but designed to look a lot older. Not being too well up on ecclesiastical terms the only facts I can glean from my encyclopaedia are that Stephen Langton, archbishop of Canterbury, was born in 1150, consecrated in 1207 and died in 1228. Also that he had a sort of running battle with bad King John.

Friday Street, known as an enchanting hamlet is a cluster of timber clad cottages along one street. At the end of the street is a large pond surrounded by lofty pines and hearty oaks.

The spirit, which in all honesty belongs more to legend than the spirit world is a young fay. Frea the fay is a lovely creature that arises from the pond on a summer's evening. It is best to avert your eyes to avoid being enticed into the water. This beckoning beauty has been responsible for the deaths of several young men. That is how the story goes anyway. Not content with their bodies the irresistible Frea demands also their spirits. That is why on a summer's night you may see the ghosts of several young men walking (or floating on air) along the street past the Stephen Langton and into the pond.

If you believe this one you'll believe anything.

PS   Did you know that King John didn't sign the Magna Carta? He could not write so the churchmen present (probably including Langton) signed it for him. He did however apply his seal at Runnymede, June 15TH 1215.

THE WHITE HART
FRIMLEY

I slipped into the White Hart the other day it has been much tastefully altered since I last used it on a regular basis. Externally little has changed except an extension of what seems to be a baronial hall. I wonder if the imbibers checking their e-mails in the front bar know that they are sitting where numerous autopsies were once carried out. Not the least of these in the early 1900's was on the body of Anne Hogg who had been bludgeoned and then had her throat cut, at her house on the A30. Her sister Caroline who also had a cut throat but survived was thought to be the culprit but nothing was ever proved. It remains one of the counties great mysteries. A far fuller account can be found in *I'll be Hanged*, by Roger Long.

The following couple of pages are from my *Caesar's Circle*.

Frimley, it would seem, is a little short of supernatural experiences. I have spent some time drinking in the local pubs, which is usually a rich source for such stories, but have come away unrewarded. I can in fact find two ghost stories of Frimley. One of which is very 'iffy' indeed. First, the better known one.

The ghost of 'Old Charlie Miles' was once a regular feature of the Old Guildford Road at Frimley. The spirit sported a deerstalker hat, a brown leather jacket and corduroy trousers tied up with string. This was Charlie's general mode of apparel. However, no country yokel was this. In life he was a retired Lieutenant Colonel who lived in Frimley Green. His spirit strolls the Old Guildford Road because it was a favourite 'haunt' of Charles before he met an untimely death in 1957.

Life had not always been good to Charlie, after retirement he and his wife bought a house in Frimley for his son, an army doctor. Unfortunately this young man was mistakenly shot by a sentry in Singapore. One factor that I have omitted to mention, is that the ghost of Charlie is always accompanied by his small brown dog; a constant companion on his earthbound perambulations.

Let us assume that the law of probability dictates that master and dog died many years apart. How does one find ones loyal canine friend on the other side. And then, project a pair of images back into the earthbound world? That is of course a rhetorical question.

As for the second Frimley ghost story, the very iffy one, I offer the reader an excerpt from a recent series I contributed to the Wokingham Times.

On a rather lighter note, there was another tale from a Tesco lady named Sue. Sue was a care assistant at Frimley Park hospital. Allegedly there was a well-related legend there in one particular ward, the cry of a wild cat foretold of an imminent death. What a lot of balderdash! Most hospitals are inundated with cats that thrive on the leftovers. Also more people die in hospitals than anywhere else. Therefore it would not seem that unusual for a patient to meet their demise while a cat miaows outside.

However, my informant relates that as she and several other impressionable young nurses were being told this story by a ward sister, a most uncanny cat like scream split the air. Whether this was purely coincidental or some third party employed to scare the living daylights out of the youngsters we shall never know. Unfortunately it is now impossible to ascertain if anybody met their maker that particular night. Incidentally, I ran over a black cat rushing to Wokingham Hospital to see the birth of my elder daughter. Enough said.

One would have thought that a village as ancient as Frimley Green would have been inundated with haunted buildings. This would seem not to be the case. One exception that proves the rule is a house called Ketton Dene in the Guildford Road. It has reputedly been haunted for years but by whom or what nobody seems to know. This is the most tenuous of associations with the supernatural and nothing has been seen, heard, experienced or imagined recently.

At the risk of repeating myself, it seems strange that the most authenticated ghost, of which Frimley Green can boast, inhabits a comparatively modern building. In the early 70's a cleaner at S C Johnson & Son Ltd was indulging in her work near the mezzanine balcony. It was late at night and the cleaning lady thought she was on her own in that part of the building. On looking up from her work the cleaner saw a tall figure, dressed in black. He seemed to be watching her. Our lady was not alarmed as she took it to be some night worker unknown to herself, but as she made to make conversation, the man disappeared.

Now somewhat more alarmed the cleaner made enquiries. Firstly had anybody been working by the mezzanine balcony that night, and, secondly had anybody else experienced the spectral watcher dressed in black. The answer to the former question was no, nobody had been working in that part of the building on that particular night. The answer to the latter question was yes; at least half a dozen people had sighted the Black Watcher, always at night and always on the balcony. And who is or was this sorrowful onlooker? There are no explanations but there are a couple of suggestions.

Before the construction of S C Johnson & Son Ltd, the site in Frimley Green was a wasteland. Overgrown farmland dotted and pebble dashed with old farm buildings in various stages of decay. Tramps used the buildings as overnight accommodation and the spectral figure is reputed to be one of the better known gentlemen of the road who often stopped there.

I do not believe this to be a plausible explanation. The point being that the spectral black onlooker is described as far younger than the tramp. So, unless one goes through a type of rejuvenation after death, this explanation would seem ridiculous. A second, more likely and also more macabre explanation is that the man in black is the ghost of a building worker who died during the construction of the building. In this case the description is far more like that of the unfortunate gentleman.

One morning recently I was having a swift one up at the White Horse (Pub With No Name) at Froxfield (see *Haunted Inns of Hampshire*) and I was chatting to a relief manageress, Chris. She had read my books and had heard me on BBC Solent. My ego was extremely well contented. Chris went on to mention that she had been a tenant at the White Hart at Frimley, in the early eighties.

"We had three ghosts there," she informed me.

"Oh yes," I replied. "I haven't heard this, but I know there were many autopsies performed there years ago."

Chris went on to explain. Ghost one, was a nun who had been caught 'frolicking' with a monk from a nearby monastery. She had been killed in the grounds of the old inn but haunted an upstairs bar. The nun or her contours had been witnessed by the ex-landlady, her husband and her staff on several occasions. She also had a habit (no pun intended) of switching on lights in this specific bar room after the door had been locked. I believe a fairly successful experiment was conducted.

Ghost two, was an old ostler, complete with white frock coat who was seen in the Stable Bar at varying times by varying people, including Chris. A nice little footnote to this story is that a Cornish girl arrived to work in the stable bar. The very first evening, before she had a chance to hear any of the White Hart's folklore, she complained that the bar was haunted. "There has been an old man in a white coat watching me for some time." Make of that what you will.

Ghost number three is far more illusive. He is a spectral Chinaman and to my knowledge the only one in the country. He has not been seen by Chris or her family but she heard the story soon after her arrival. Apparently the Chinaman worked in the kitchen in the late 19TH century. There was a brawl followed by a knife fight and the death of the little oriental. Legend dictates that his mourning family removed the body and it's destination never discovered.

Congratulations to the White Hart for the first Chinese takeaway in the country. I must refrain from flippancy.

THE KINGS ARMS & ROYAL HOTEL
GODALMING

The Kings Arms has a flourishing wealth of stories. Being set in Godalming High Street it was obviously a coaching inn. Its geographical position, almost half way between London and the swiftly growing port of Portsmouth made it a favourite of travellers. The Kings Arms was frequented by such awesome figures as Henry VIII and Lord Nelson. At the other end of the scale however it was a convenient place to lodge French prisoners of war, and later, British felons on their way to be deported. In 1698 the Kings Arms entertained its most famous guest, Czar Peter the Great of Russia. The landlord, James Moon, was at first delighted at the prospect but as the days went by he began to realise that the Czar's boisterous and rowdy entourage had no intention of paying for their vitals, or the vast damages caused by wild parties. God-fearing Godalming folk began to avoid the High Street like the plague. Young men were set upon and young wenches deflowered.

Leaving Godalming the Czar's entourage moved on to Deptford to inflict themselves upon the hospitality of the diarist John Evelyn. Evelyn suffered some of Moon's experiences but to a far greater degree. The party were with him for 3 months and did immeasurable damage. They were described by Evelyn's bailiff as 'right nasty people'.

No doubt Peter the Great enjoyed his stay at the Kings Arms because his phantom is still thought to reside there. The ghost manifests itself by kicking off his boots between 1am and 2am. It is said to be a most disturbing sound.

Other Godalming stories are: -

The little town of Godalming has two very strange stories. One is the 'Rabbit Woman' and the other concerns Westbrook House.

The Rabbit Woman was one Mary Tofts, who in 1727 declared she had given birth to between 18 and 24 baby rabbits. Mary's excuse was that she had been scared by a rabbit whilst pregnant. Her charade was clever enough to convince Mr Howard, a Guildford surgeon who had been present at the supposed birth and Dr St André, the royal physician.

Mary Tofts motive for the fraud was that she hoped to gain a royal pension. In the face of much ridicule Mary withdrew her claim and received a short prison sentence. The famous doctors hoped that their embarrassment would be short lived. However they hoped in vain. Hogarth did a cartoon on the subject showing Mary lying on her bed in much discomfort whilst a host of small rabbits ran from the bottom of her skirt. So our Mary remains to this day immortalised for posterity by one of England's greatest artists.

The Meath Home once Westbrook House belonged to the family of Oglethorpe. They were stoic supporters of the Stuart cause. Just before James II was deposed in 1688 in favour of William of Orange his queen gave birth to a son. He was known to the Jacobites as James III but to the Hannovians as the Old Pretender. James being an inconvenience to the throne was forced to spend most of his life in exile. Stuart hopes died with James in 1766. However legend has it that he was not of royal birth at all. The baby born to Queen Mary in 1688 died at birth, as had several other of the unfortunate Queen. The story goes that the recently born son of Sir Theophilus Oglethorpe was smuggled in to the Palace of Westminster in a warming pan and exchanged for the dead royal baby.

We shall never know.

Westbrook House has a Stuart ghost thought to be that of Bonnie Prince Charlie who surreptitiously met with his supporters here just before the rising of 1745. As the Prince was in hiding he took his exercise in the grounds of Westbrook in the evenings, usually attired in a long brown cloak. It is therefore reasonable to assume that the phantom often witnessed at twilight is that of the Bonnie Prince.

In the 1950's-60's there was a plethora of sightings of a ghostly nun at Westbrook. She was however only seen from the back, always at twilight, dressed in a brown habit and with long curling hair. One does not have to be Sherlock Holmes to suspect that the two figures are one and the same.

Godalming. Ghosts of Lammas Lands.

This is not a book on murders. I've written three on murders and they sold in their dozens. So I shall be brief.

On November 11TH 1817 George Chennell senior a kindly and generous old man was found dead at his home in Godalming High Street. George senior had a shoemakers and cartage business next to the Little George.

The well-respected man was found in his bedroom, his head had been crushed with blows from a blunt instrument and his throat had been cut. The body of his housekeeper of over 30 years Elizabeth Wilson was found in the kitchen. Her skull had been fractured and her throat had also been cut. Readers who wish further details of this horrific double murder should obtain a copy of *Surrey Murders* by John Janaway. For this account, suffice it to say, that after much circumstantial evidence and several witnessed actions, George Chennell junior, 38 year old son of the deceased, and William Chalcraft, 51, a ne'er-do-well, who did occasional work for the deceased were charged with the crimes.

There is little doubt after reading the case that both men were guilty as sin. A third person, who was arrested but later discharged in a deal that demanded her giving evidence for the prosecution was their look-out, Sarah Hurst.

After hearing the evidence at Guildford's Guildhall, it took the jury just three minutes to find the pair guilty. On August 14TH 1818 Chennell and Chalcraft were taken by cart from Guildford prison to the Lammas Lands, near the church and River Wey at Godalming. From this same cart the hangman launched them both into eternity. Both men pleaded their innocence until the last.

And still on a summer's night they say that a churning cart is heard in the vicinity of Lammas Lands. The distinct sound of a murmuring crowd can also be heard. And then – complete silence – broken only by the gnawing sound of rope on wood as two heavy objects sway in the breeze.

St. MARYS CHURCHYARD, EWELL
Beware of scruffy beggar children playing hide and seek amid the gravestones.
They were plague victims from London who were interred here

BOURNE MILL, FARNHAM
Once a drinking club that is haunted by a maid.

BOURNE MILL, FARNHAM
The nearby gardens where you wouldn't want to spend the night

THE BUSH, FARNHAM
Haunted by an ex-maid

STEPHEN LANGTON, FRIDAY STREET

Local Lad made good. Stephen Langton became Archbishop of Canterbury. Be Careful that a spirit Doesn't tempt you in to a nearby lake.

THE WHITE HART, FRIMLEY

Once used for autopsies and inquests, this has at least three distinct ghosts

THE KINGS ARMS & ROYAL HOTEL, GODALMING

The spirit of Peter the Great, Czar of Russia is loathe to leave here.

THE ANGEL, GUILDFORD

The ghost of the Prince Imperial stood obligingly still whilst a guest drew his likeness

THE KINGS ARMS, EAST MOLESEY
This has several ghosts and a chair that will not lie down

TAGG ISLAND, HAMPTON
Where Tommy Hann, the Brooklands racing driver's car slipped from a ferry. A lady friend of his was drowned. Did she appear to a nearby resident?

THE GREYHOUND, LINGFIELD

A ghostly schoolboy dressed in grey is blamed for purloining small items

THE CROWN, OLD OXTED

A drop in temperature followed by footsteps are the symptoms of the Crown's
haunting

LOSLEY HOUSE

This grandiose estate is not really Godalming. It is nearer to Compton and therefore does not really qualify. Losely House was built from stones of demolished Waverley Abbey. In the early days it was owned by Sir William More and had connections with Queen Elizabeth and James I.

Losley has a plethora of ghosts. Three well known, two not so well known and one best left alone. The three well known are – the nice lady, the nasty lady and a child (gender unknown). The nice lady resembles a portrait in the attic. Clad in Victorian attire she only appears when her picture is removed. She is reported to have a pleasant smiling face.

The nasty lady is far less pleasant. She is stern and scowling. Tradition dictates that she murdered her son/daughter (ghost number 3) by drowning him/her in the moat that was once a feature of the house. The lesser-known ghosts, rarely seen are a phantom coach and horses, seen near the main entrance, and a Victorian couple that wander the grounds. But what of ghost number six? What terrifying spectre chased an American tenant and her party from Losely in 1913? The tenant a Miss Dodge would not set foot in the place again. None of the party would return. We shall never know why. They were all sworn to secrecy and none of them ever broke the vow.

A true fairy story.

Long, long ago and far-a-way (3 miles south-west of Godalming) there stood a 'palace', not a very striking 'palace' more of a manor house actually. And in this 'palace' lived a very wealthy eccentric king. He could move heavens and earth (at least four lakes, two hills and a forest). He built an underground 'palace' which one entered from a door set in a far-a-way tree. Not the far-a-way tree of Enid Blyton's Silky, Moonbeam, Dame Washerlot etc. but a hollow holly tree.

On entering, one found oneself in a small room with a slanting underground ramp taking one even further into the subterranean depths. Other rooms and staircases follow ever deeper and deeper until a canal emerges. That is correct, a canal, far beneath the first lake. A boat has been provided, cast off, there is a speck of light at the end of the tunnel. Eventually the tide will take you to a second lake and an intriguing small island. Disembark here, the island, though small, is big enough to hold a small dance band and that is exactly what its purpose was. Further steps down will bring you to a glass-domed ballroom. Here local 'princesses' waltzed the night away and watched exotic fish play through the glass sides and roof and everybody lived happily ever after.

Well no, not quite.

The owner of this fantastic 'palace' was Whitaker Wright, an entrepreneur and self-made millionaire several times over. He spent a million and a quarter constructing the underwater ballroom and improving his nearby estate by building lakes, forests, hills and follies. It was said by all that he was a charming, romantic and generous man.

Unfortunately for Mr Whitaker Wright he was brought before the authorities and charged with fraud. Convicted, he was sentenced to seven years. But this lover of life, this extrovert, was not the type of man to languish in prison. He committed suicide by swallowing cyanide before leaving the Old Bailey.

The 'palace' has gone. The park remains but has PRIVATE notices on its many gatehouses. The lake remains and so probably does the ballroom. It was there in the early eighties, and yours truly is endeavouring to find out more at the time of writing. Locals seem a little tight-lipped on the subject. Perhaps they are wary of the ghost of Whitaker Wright who is reputed still to wander around the estate he so loved in life.

STOP PRESS

In early November I made some local enquiries about the underwater ballroom. According to a much-respected historian, the ballroom is still there, in excellent condition but bureaucratically inaccessible.

THE ANGEL
GUILDFORD

The hauntings at the Angel are quite well attested and also often but not well reported. The inn is a perfect venue for ghosts. It is the oldest in Guildford, nobody knows just how old. It is in the cobbled High Street a long stones throw from the castle, to which a subterranean tunnel is thought to exist. There is/was a priest hole in a front bedroom and a bullet was discovered in an old beam. A less authenticated tunnel is said to lead to St Mary's church.

The Prince Imperial (the heir apparent in the French empire of Napoleon) stayed here in 1876, occupying a large double front room, which has since been named after him. In the opinions of some it is this noble gentleman who haunts the room, but more of that later.

Hauntings and phantoms according to many reports started in the late 60's or early 70's. I totally disagree with this as I have heard reports from locals and employees who have experienced strange happenings from the 50's, 40's and even the 30's. Reports probably go back as far or beyond living memory.

There have been reports of 'something in room 3' since the mid-sixties, what it is no one is sure. 'The Something' carries with it a deep feeling of depression and fear. The presence was once quite regularly reported but seems to have subsided of late. Room 1, the Prince Imperial's Room, has a more concise story. In 1969 a switchboard operator saw a guests warning light on her board, it came from room 1, the Imperial Prince's room. On opening the door she found the lady occupant frozen with fear. Too shocked in fact to impart any information but whatever it was she saw apparently came from the mirror.

It was the same mirror in the same room that brought a second sighting in 1970. A guest and his wife saw in the mirror a gentleman sporting a bold moustache and dressed in old fashioned military uniform, thought to be French. Obviously it was later deduced that this was the spirit of the Imperial Prince. Personally I don't see why it should as any number of military gentlemen might have used the room over the years.

I have read reports of this sighting that suggest that the phantom appeared for some twenty minutes to half an hour. Total balderdash. I think to my recollection that the general period of a ghost's appearance is about 30-50 seconds; 2 minutes would be exceptionally long. What else is strange is that the guest that experienced this spirit made a sketch of it on a serviette with a ballpoint pen. He stated that he had no time to find anything else.

One would have thought that with 30 minutes at his disposal he would have found at least half a dozen witnesses and a decent drawing pad. This is not to say that I disbelieve this encounter, it is to say that I think the length of the performance was grossly exaggerated.

Guildford has everything for a town; a castle, shops, a plethora of pubs and a hoard of ghosts. Here are a few more stories, starting with a mystery.

Since time began alchemists have sought the ability of turning other minerals into gold. In 1782 a respected Guildford scientist believed he had accomplished this feat. On moving from London to Stoke, near Guildford, James Price had found in a drawer a 'recipe' for making gold. Price, at 30, had honours from the Fellowship of the Royal Society and an honours degree from Oxford. He took a small estate at Stoke, which had once been owned by a Dr Irish, a mad magician and a recluse who had died under suspicious circumstances. Irish had a well-fitted laboratory at the house, which had attracted Price to the abode. Price found some old papers of Irish's, which stated that he had been visited by a ghost who had left him some substances and a promise that he (Irish) could construct the purest of gold. I have yet to hear of a ghost who could transport solid materials, but I shall not spoil the story. I shall however cut it short.

Price put Irish's notes and materials into much use for a number of days, finally shouting to his fiancé "Eureka, I have produced pure gold!" or words to that effect. Over the following months Price's miracle was witnessed by many well respected scientists. Using mercury, a mysterious red powder and various other ingredients he would amaze the most sceptical of audiences. Many official tests were made on the gold, which without exception proved successfully conclusive. The Royal Society embarrassed and incredulous at one of its member's claims decided to take action. Price was invited to lay his discovery before his colleagues for a final investigation into his claims. Weeks turned into months but Price did not attend various appointments to satisfy the Royal Society and to substantiate his name in history. Suspicious murmurs arose and witnesses began to doubt their own testimonies. Disconcerting rumours of Price screaming like a madman and threatening violence were rife. Publicly Price stated that he had used up all the red powder and that to produce more would be highly dangerous to his health. He certainly did not look well, he had aged considerably and his body jerked with nervous spasms.

Two honourable members of the Royal Society, Sir Philip Clarke and Dr Spence went down to Guildford to offer Price an ultimatum. Prove your statements or face professional disgrace. On reaching the house in August

1783 they were met by Price who agreed to show the distinguished pair an experiment to produce gold. The experiment went horribly wrong; Price had used the last of the mysterious red powder. Seeing that all was in vain and that the powder could not be reproduced without his probable death during the process, Price reached for a bottle of prussic acid and downed it. Three hours later he was dead. Price's death left many questions unanswered. One, what was the strange red powder? Not a trace of it was ever found. Two, what happened to the formula? Had Price destroyed it? Three, why the madness and the rapid aging? Four, it is an accepted fact that the transmutation of base metals into gold is absolutely impossible but why so many witnesses including assaying specialists that were so convinced of the product?

With hindsight most of the questions can be answered or at least a plausible theory put forward. Most informed scientists now agree that the mysterious red powder was wholly or mostly arsenic. The other main metal was, as we know, mercury. Nearly all the mercury in the late 18TH century was imported from the continent where it was a closely guarded secret, that a small amount of gold was used as a preservative. Price was probably made ill by the constant use of arsenic and his mind was affected by the regular use of mercury. Mercury was at one time used in the making of hats; it was rubbed over the coating to give the headpiece a sheen. Factory workers who had spent years at this practice absorbed quantities through their skin. This in turn affected their minds. Hence the phrase 'As mad as a hatter'.

Back to Price. It appears that he had in fact been extracting gold from the mercury when he thought, in all sincerity, that he had been creating it. Valentine Dyall, that wonderful man of mysteries in the 50's put forward a very plausible theory. At great detriment to his own health Price had processed a small amount of red powder, mercury and other substances to show to Sir Philip Clarke and Dr Spence. One of these fine scholars might have pointed out to Price that his formula was not a transmutation but merely an extraction. If this was the case imagine Price's reaction. He had destroyed his physical and mental health extracting gold rather than creating it. Sick in mind and fearful of being ridiculed by the scientific world, he took his own life. And what of the phantom that brought the formula to Price's predecessor Dr Irish? Take that story with a pinch of arsenic.

YORK ROAD CAR PARK
GUILDFORD

There is a slight difference of opinion as to the vocation of the grey lady that haunts the multi-storey car park. In 1969 two workmen who were helping to complete the building witnessed a lady in grey on one of the upper levels.

The traditional story is that she was a young Quaker girl named Lorna. Lorna is said to have died some 200 years ago. Her father, a devout Quaker, found his daughter in the arms of a man of a different faith. In his rage he ousted his daughter from the house. In blind panic Lorna fled. She tripped and fell headlong into a chalk pit; unfortunately dying of her injuries. The father was unrepentant, forbidding his daughter to be buried in the family grave. It is thought that the car park is built on the actual chalk pit where destiny did for Lorna. Personally I cannot see why her spirit should strive for the upper floors of the building.

A second account has the grey lady as the spirit of a nun who was murdered in the chalk quarry. After some experiences in the 1960's and 1970's it was decided that the earthbound nun should be exorcised. Here was the rub. The Catholics decided that she was one of their order and the Anglican Church decided she was a protestant and that they should perform the exorcism. Thanks to the great British compromise, the grey lady (Lorna or the nun) was duly exorcised twice.

MERROW Nr GUILDFORD

In 1977 there were a series of articles in the Surrey Advertiser concerning strange goings on in a council house in Merrow near Guildford. There were three generations of the family in the house. The daughter of the tenant and her husband heard screams coming from the bedroom of their two year old son. As they rushed into the child's room they saw the child pointing into the corner of the room and shouting "That's not my daddy, take him away." This could have been put down to a childish nightmare if other members of the family had not already witnessed a man in ancient attire slinking in other corners of the house. The couple had another very young child at the time and after several attempts at exorcism the family moved away.

Joan Foreman in her book *The Haunted South* mentions this case and states that the haunted building was thought to be on the site of a gallows where a highwayman was once hanged. Personally I am always a little sceptical of the precise position of long lost gallows, there are few if any records kept. But generally they were at the crossroads of thoroughfares to obtain the maximum impact on passing travellers.

Still in Merrow. A local highwayman who doubled as a coachman was one James Potter. Potter worked at the nearby White Hart Inn but between being coachman and potman he managed to rob many of the gentry that passed through the area. Potter was convicted of stealing eleven guineas and a watch. He was sentenced to death with two other local villains a pair of violent burglars Christopher Ellis and Frederick William Gregg. Gregg was especially known for his gratuitous violence. In August 1776 the three were hanged on Ganghill Common after spending much time in prayer and advising the vast crowd against loose women.
A spectral highwayman (well at least a spectral man on a horse) was witnessed on many occasions before the area was developed. Speculation was rife as to which of the three blaguards had returned to an earthbound existence. As mentioned in an earlier chapter not every phantom horseman is necessarily a highwayman. Every ghost with a French cocked hat need not be Claude Duval. Of the three the most likely candidate is thought to be Potter. The other two were footpads in every sense of the word.

A.A. BUILDING

Guildford's massive AA building was once haunted by a rather zealous cleaning lady. Seldom but occasionally sighted in an old fashioned wrap around apron, this busy lady was often heard emptying ashtrays, sweeping, dusting and occasionally flushing the toilets. Her diligent actions were more than a little disconcerting for the night staff but thankfully the industrious woman finally took her retirement.

CLANDON PARK
GUILDFORD

Clandon Park was built in the 1730's by Giacomo Leoni, a Venetian architect who combined Baroque, Palladian and European styles. The parkland was laid out by Capability Brown and includes a parterre, a grotto and an unusual New Zealand Maori house. The beautiful old building close to the Pilgrims Way has encouraged several of out great poets to wax lyrical, Rudyard Kipling and William Watson included.

An unknown grave beside the main gates contains the remains of a man who saw the execution of Charles Stuart (not a lot of people know that). Clandon Park has an obligatory grey lady but I shall not enlarge upon the fact, because, in all honesty I know nothing more.

Nick Brazil in his inspired book *A Journey with Ghosts* tells of a friend of his who experienced some strange phenomena here. But as it is more of a 'time warp' experience rather than an actual ghost story I shall go no further. Readers should either buy Nick's book or visit Clandon. Both are enjoyable experiences and who knows it may just happen to you.

A quick one to close with. Long ago at Guildford Grammar School a young pupil saw the spectre of his fathers groom enter an empty room. Knowing the man well the boy followed and watched the groom disappear before his eyes. The following day he got a message that the groom had died at the precise time of his spirits appearance. What can one say? There are thousands of similar unprovable stories. Another from the vanishing hitch-hiker syndrome.

KINGS ARMS
HAMPTON

I heard about the hauntings at the Kings Arms, East Molesey, by a very roundabout route. In 1999 I wrote a book called *Haunted Pubs of Hampshire*, in it I included the Chequers at Well, which I first discovered on the TV programme The Village. In the early part of 2001 BBC Southern Counties contacted me to do a series of programmes on haunted pubs. I included the Chequers and did an interview over the phone with a lady called Denise. After our conversation Denise informed me that when she worked at the Kings Arms in Hampton there were some very strange happenings indeed. Therefore on a beautiful unique June morning I introduced myself to the landlord Tim Hain.

"Ghosts," said Tim, "How many do you want?"

"How many have you got?" says I.

I mentioned to Tim that I had already been talking to his very attractive barmaid and she had told me that no way could anybody induce her to go down the middle cellar.

"The middle cellar," said Tim, "is probably the only room in the building that isn't supposed to be haunted. Let us see how many we have. The function room has an inexplicable burst of cold air. There is supposed to be the ghost of a boy in the garden who jumped from a second floor window to commit suicide, possible after finding his mother dead, after hanging herself. She may or may not be the lady that haunts the right hand cellar."

I was surprised to learn that these events had been as recent as the early 1940's. Incidentally the window from which the boy jumped has for some reason been bricked up.

"Anything else" I asked.

"There is something in the third cellar which seems to be benign but playful. There is a grey lady who looks out from an upstairs window. I have seen her when walking in Bushey Park. Also a chair that rights itself in the cellar where the first suicide was."

Tim asked me if I would like to inspect the cellars. Neither of the two I inspected seemed to be in use, other than as junk rooms. The middle cellar was reached by a type of wooden ladder from near the bottom of the stairs. There was no light provided and Tim's torch needed a battery. We went by striking matches. How much the atmosphere of oppression was contributed to by the lack of light, old furniture, broken staring old portraits and the many cobwebs that brushed ones face I do not know. What I do know is that had I been the barmaid (Louise) I should not have been keen to frequent it.

The second cellar had a poor light but was in much the same condition. Tim pointed to a broken chair. "That's the one that stood up many times after we laid it down. We even nailed it down once with no effect."

Could this be I wondered the chair the young mother had stood on prior to hanging herself. We shall never know.

I climbed out of the second cellar. I found it far more oppressive than the first.

"Would you sleep down there?" I asked Tim.

"Not flippin' likely" was his reply, or words of that ilk.

I wondered to myself why I had worn a clean white shirt, which was now black and new navy trousers that were now white.

"Is that all?" I asked, brushing myself down.

"There is one more thing," Tim said. "There's a something upstairs that throws things about."

"Mild poltergeist activity," I asked.

"Yes, I believe that's what you call it. It throws salt and pepper pots. Oh, and its favourite is candlesticks."

"How often does this happen?" I enquired.

"Oh, about a couple of times a week."

My final question was to find out if Tim was intimidated by all these spirits. He replied in the negative adding that his unsolicited guests were quite a friendly bunch.

I went away in deep thought.

HAMPTON VILLAGE

The Royal ghosts of Hampton Court are too overdone and numerous to mention.

An attractive old house on the river at Hampton was once inhabited and then haunted by Nell Gwyn. In the 1930's a new maid told her mistress how she had seen a beautiful woman wearing a low cut dress. Asking her maid if she was frightened, the lady of the house was assured that she was not. The maid replied that the atmosphere was so serene that she was disappointed when the figure disappeared. With a touch of inspiration the mistress brought out a photograph she owned of Nell Gwyn's portrait at Hampton Court Palace. "That's the lady," agreed the maid.

The lady of the house mentioned above was affected several times by strange occurrences. Soon after buying the property she and her husband were out in their punt on the river. Looking towards their garden and at a particularly splendid magnolia tree, they saw, what they thought was the shadow of a struggling man hanging from one of the branches. On leaving their punt and hurrying to the splendid magnolia they found nothing amiss. Several days later the husband was socialising at a club when he met and introduced himself to a nearby neighbour. "Oh, you are the new people at X," he said. "An unlucky house that, the gardener hanged himself on the magnolia tree a few years ago."

The third strange happening at the attractive unlucky house also happened in the late 1930's. The above mentioned lady awoke early one morning and leaning on her balcony she noticed three figures, two men and a woman. All were wet and distraught but the lady being held by the two men was obviously in a poor condition. Before the lady on the balcony could offer assistance all three figures disappeared. A few minutes later the lady's maid brought her breakfast in.

"Have you heard?" she asked her mistress. "There has been a terrible accident at the Tagg Island Ferry. A car slipped into the water, two men were saved but the lady died."

Let me tell you a little about Fred Karno his army and Tagg Island.

Fred Karno, real name Frederick Westcott, was born in Exeter in 1866. After several poorly paid jobs including a plumber's mate, Fred started his showbiz career by being a gymnast or acrobat. Fred and two others became The Three Carnos and later Fred Karno's Army. Working with people like Charlie Chaplin and Harry Weldon, Fred became a very rich man and popular on both sides of the Atlantic. In 1912 Fred Karno bought Tagg Island a scruffy place in the middle of the Thames near Hampton. Tagg Island had been the home of local gypsies for generations. Fred moved them off incurring many curses whilst doing so. The travellers were in the way of Karno's project. A millionaire's playground with a hotel, ballroom, restaurant, theatre and splendid gardens. Fred went bankrupt in 1926, probably through outlandish investments rather than any gypsy's curse. He owed £16,000, a vast sum in those days. Fred had not lost his comic genius but he was aging rapidly. After his wife died in 1927 he married his mistress of 25 years, Marie Moore. Fred Karno the music hall king died in obscurity at his off license in Dorset. In his will he left £42.

Fred's paradise island, Karisino (Tagg Island) was still the place to be seen during the late 20's and 30's. A man often seen there was the famous Brooklands motorist Tommy Hann. In 1923 and 1924 Hann took everything before him but by the 1930's Tommy was a has-been. Now working as an experimental engineer Tommy put all of his money into a car that he practically built himself. It was a dismal failure. Soon after, the racing driver was found gassed in his flat in Holland Park Avenue.

Tommy Hann had confided in friends that he had lost his nerve after his friend's wife had died at Tagg Island when their car had slipped off of the ferry. Although they had dived many times the wife of his best friend had died. It had affected him badly.

Remember our lady from the big house with the magnolia tree. When she read of Tommy Hann's death in her daily paper and saw his photograph with his friends, she checked the date of the incident. Of course she was right. There was no mistaking the three spirits she had witnessed from her window. Tommy and his friend, very damp but alive, and the poor lady between them who had died.

Make of this what you will.

THE HOLLY & LAUREL?
BOTTLE & GLASS?
HOLMWOOD

Holmwood stands on the A24 London to Worthing road. It was an obvious old staging route. The village was the one time home of Alfred Gwynne Vanderbilt one of the rich and famous New York Vanderbilts. Alfred's money helped in the upkeep of the road and he used to revel in driving his coach and horses down it at great speed. Unfortunately for philanthropy he died bravely on the Lusitania in the Great War.

Holmwood Common, where wild boars had been hunted since time immemorial, was thought by King James II, who hunted here regularly, to boast the largest stags in England. Where there is good hunting you will find lawless squatters and footpads. Holmwood Common had such people in abundance. One large and untamed family was said to have relatives in Ashdown forest. When things became too hot for them, they just swapped places thereby making recognition extremely difficult and totally confusing the authorities. Holmwood was sufficiently close to the sea and lawless enough to make it an attractive venue for smugglers transporting goods to the capital.

'The Bottle and Glass?' was an ideal venue for providing storage and alibis. Standing as it did on the main coaching route. Its claim to be haunted is a little obscure and I obtained it third hand. It seems that a horseman at the inn was scared by the spectre of a massive Australian aborigine. His horse bolted throwing him to the ground and breaking his neck. It is said to be the galloping hooves that are heard on some winter nights. But what? I ask, became of the spectral giant aborigine, he seems far more interesting.

It is my rule to set out and visit every inn that I write about. After half a day searching the Holmwood area I could not find where it was standing or even where it had stood. I took my life in my hand flittering across the A24 visiting North Holmwood, Mid Holmwood and South Holmwood.

Nobody didn't know nuffin.

I asked postmen, garagemen, shopkeepers etc. etc. I drew a blank. Finally I was directed to a gentleman who had lived in South Holmwood for a lifetime. He informed me that there had only been one pub in the three villages and that was the Holly and Laurel, and that was now closed. I had been past the building several times. It was now a collection of small businesses and called the Emporium. A small part to the side still had the Holly and Laurel sign. It was, to say in its favour, right on the lie of the old coaching route. So there you have it. No Bottle and Glass has ever been known in Holmwood. Does the ex Holly and Laurel feel right? Yes it does. Was a horseman thrown here at the sight of a gigantic spectral aborigine? Please yourself.

THE ROSE AND CROWN
KENLEY

It is a wonder to me that this old pub has remained very little altered over the years. It is still a greater surprise that it has kept its name. Unfortunately this area, like my own East Berks, is prone to be 'advanced' and 'modernised' by the great conglomerates. I quite expected to see a Rat and Parrot, a Littern Tree or some other Firkin silly name awaiting me.

The Rose and Crown is on an old staging route, horse drawn coaches were once a common sight as they conveyed people from the capital to Lewes, Newhaven and Eastbourne. Though extremely busy during the day it was not many years ago when the evening shadows brought a rather austere solemnity. The winding hill and the vast disused chalk pit only endorsed the feeling.

Is it surprising that there are reports of a ghostly dark coach here? Jet black horses gallop through the night pulling their passengers and their distraught driver towards inevitable doom. Obviously out of control the phantom coach passes the inn at a ferocious speed and then completely vanishes. There was a fatal coach accident here in the 1870's. It is supposedly well documented. The driver having lost control was killed along with several passengers.

Near to Kenley once stood a medieval village that boasts a grey lady.

Kenley, grey lady.

Yet another wronged nun is this. Reportedly seen in the early evening carrying a bundle that is purported to be a baby. In 1966 a dig was organised to unearth the medieval village that had virtually decomposed. The village of Waddington thrived during the 9TH century. The chapel finally being burnt down in he 1780's. The 60's dig was quite successful, apart from revealing ancient walls some people are of the opinion it permitted the grey lady to escape. Was the poor woman entombed alive for some transgression, is the proof of this indiscretion the bundle in her arms..........we shall never know.

Here is another little story concerning Kenley.

In 1920 Eric Toombe a 30 year old son of the Reverend Gordon Toombe of Enstone, Oxfordshire, set up business at Welcomes Farm, Hayes Lane, Kenley, with a rather dicey character named Ernest Dyer. In 1921 Toombe disappeared, his body could not be discovered and the police were getting nowhere with Dyer, whom they suspected.

In 1921 the farmhouse caught fire and was razed to the ground. Once again Dyer was suspected, once again the evidence was not sufficient.

In 1922 the police had Dyer 'dead to rights' on a fraud charge. He disappeared but was traced to the north east coast where an attempt was made to arrest him at a Scarborough hotel. Dyer drew a revolver and in the ensuing melee received a fatal shot to the brain. Further research on the police's behalf uncovered the fact that in 1921 Dyer had drawn £1350 from Toombe's Paris bank account using Toombe's passport and forging his signature.

In 1923 Toombe's mother dreamed that her son had been shot in the head and that his body was lying in a cesspool at Welcomes Farm. This turned out to be the case and the dream was thought to be a supernatural revelation.

Personally I am not so sure if one considers the law of probability; the farm was the most likely venue for the body and the cesspool the most likely place on the farm. This is a something or nothing case.

THE GREYHOUND INN
LINGFIELD

It is a pity, nay a blessing, that so many people visit the all weather racing track and so few the village. Within a couple of hundred yards one may see the Old Cage Inn, boasting of its nativity in 1592. The actual Old Cage gaol that once housed poachers, drunkards and other miscreants. Alongside which stands the inevitable village duck pond and the largest hollowest oak I have ever seen. Then of course there is the Greyhound.

The Greyhound Inn has been around since the 1570's. The ghost here is a little inept for such surroundings. Over the years small objects have disappeared, not an unusual occurrence in any household. A well respected clairvoyant was called in and described the spirit as a young boy in a grey suit. Other than a feeling of sudden cold there is little else to report. I believe there is more here and given the time I should like to investigate further.

Whilst in Lingfield it would be an idea to pop down to Puttendon Manor.

PUTTENDON MANOR
LINGFIELD

Now for a ghost story of little evidence but one that has been elaborated on, on many occasions. Puttendon Manor is an exceptionally attractive house, so much so that it is regularly seen as the backdrop in films, TV commercials and documentaries. It was built as a moated manor in 1477 by Reginald Sondes. The Sondes family finally obtained a title and Sir George Sondes became Earl of Faversham in 1676. Sondes two sons from his first marriage lived in constant jealous competition. Finally the younger son killed the elder (the heir) in a fit of jealousy. What happened to the perpetrator we are not told but must assume that justice prevailed, for it was a mother grieving her two sons that planted two weeping ash trees in their memory. It was reported (probably twaddle) that good luck would stay with the building whilst the trees existed.

It is not however the weeping mother whose spirit remains at Puttendon Manor. It is another lady of long residence. She seems to be a benign creature. The lady is rarely seen, I believe just once in the massive bedroom. It is the sound of the rustle of silk that is more familiar and occasionally her footsteps followed by a whiff of exotic perfume. Workmen staying in the master bedroom during extensions witnessed the aural rustle, the footsteps and the aroma. Another workman painting the stairs experienced the same symptoms. I wonder if a ghost brushed against wet paint would any attach itself to the spectre. No I am not being flippant or facetious. If some ghosts are of sufficient physical manifestation to unlock drawers and open doors, why should they not pick up wet paint or even carry drops of water after walking through ponds.

To return to the factual. The owner in the 1960's discovered a store of decorative hats and a vast number of perfume bottles. This would seem to go along with the habits of the sweetly benign spectral lady.

There is a second ghost at Puttendon Manor, he is neither seen nor heard, he is however smelt! An aroma of pipe smoke comes from this gentleman's old armchair. He is thought to be the exotic lady's husband, for what logical reason I do not know. Could it be assumed, I wonder, that the lady perfumed herself to banish the smell of pipe smoke. Or, could it be that the gentleman lit his pipe to save being asphyxiated by the strongly aromatic perfume.

THE ROEBUCK, RICHMOND
The spectacular view from the Roebuck

THE HOLE IN THE WALL, RICHMOND
Haunt of the Victorians most evil woman

THE TALBOT, RIPLEY

Reputedly haunted by a drunken coachman who fell to his death down the stairs

THE CASTLE RESTAURANT, SUNBURY
(now CAFÉ ROUGE)

The Café Rouge was the scene of a brawl by Cromwell's soldiers A barmaid who lost her life in the affray is said to haunt the ladies toilet. There is no point locking the door she can walk through walls

THE CRICKETERS
(now FIELDER & FIRKIN), SUTTON
Said to be haunted by a refined lady cricketer who died in the bar

THE DONKEY, TILFORD
Where a phantom donkey makes an ass of himself

THE GOLDEN GROVE, TWYNERSH
Supposedly haunted by a young girl murdered at the inn.

St. ANNE'S HILL, TWYNERSH
The very eerie springhead at St. Anne's Hill. Just to the right of the picture, could that be a cowled figure?

THE WHEATSHEAF, VIRGINIA WATER

A vision of a tragedy came to a man staying here, a vision that unfortunately came true

THE GROTTO , WEYBRIDGE

The subterranean passage to Oatlands is now blocked and the sighs and murmurings
are no longer heard

THE SHIP, WEYBRIDGE
Did the ghost of a man who committed suicide slip in from next door during alterations?

THE GRANTLEY ARMS, WONERSH
An otherwise friendly monk detests Christmas and pulls down the decorations

THE CROWN
OLD OXTED

Years ago one had ample time to view this romantic old town whilst stuck on the A25 in one enormous traffic jam. However, having spent some three hours worming ones way through Guildford, Dorking, Reigate, Redhill and Bletchingly one was not always in the frame of mind to be appreciative.

Thank God for the M25, with all its faults. Also Old Oxted should thank its lucky stars for the by-pass that has left it alone and intact. What a beautiful place to live with four interesting pubs in approximately 200 yards. Even the Chef and Brewer sign at the Bell seems to be in keeping. Of the others, The George, The Wheatsheaf and The Crown look as though they are part of a film set. Even the colourful bag-woman climbing the hill pushing her garments in a supermarket trolley looked part of a pre-cast scene.

The Crown, arguable the most attractive pub in the town, has a cold room suspected of being haunted. Andrew Green tells of one landlord who reported that the atmosphere was so physically chilling that his breath could be seen leaving his mouth. There would seem to be no substantiated story here, no slayings, buried alive nuns or distraught madmen. I did enquire as to why The Crown was called 'The Original Tree House' but the barmaid didn't seem to know that it was. However, the sudden drop in temperature seems quite well attested to; as do the heavy footsteps that reverberate to the cottage next door.

That's about it.

ROYAL OAK
PURLEY

Another choked area on the roads running south from the capital.

I am told that this pub has been slightly removed from its original position. It does not look particularly old at this moment in time. It is now almost part of a large complex in this least interesting part of Surrey. The Royal Oak has a friendly ghost, a little old man who once worked at an old market garden situated opposite the inn. In life he used to come across to chatter to the tram drivers that frequented the Royal Oak. Recent witnesses of this benign spirit describe him as an elderly gentleman with a stoop who leans on his stick in the bar.

THE ROEBUCK
RICHMOND HILL, RICHMOND

The Roebuck is quite an unpretentious little pub. It nestles between its more austere and grandiose neighbours. The massive Richmond Gate and Richmond Hill hotels stand here, as do the Wick and Wick House (described later). From this position the view is staggering. A board points out Ham House, what's left of Richmond Palace and further away Hampton Court and even Windsor Castle on a very clear day. Myself I like to wander a little way down and view Glovers Island from the Victorian Gothic splendour of the Petersham Hotel.

Back to The Roebuck. Andrew Green's *Our Haunted Kingdom*, tells us that Pope had a garden here and supposedly nurtured the oldest weeping willow in Europe. The Roebuck's ghost is/was an unspecified customer. Apparently the apparition is so life like that a friend of the landlords asked for the keys to let the 'customer' out.

This spectral customer might or might not be connected with a pillar of translucent mist that appeared in a bedroom in the 70's. It certainly put the frights up the occupants, two local policemen. The officers, men one would have thought used to recording details, described the mist as being the height of an average man. They also describe a significant drop in temperature. The figure then moved towards the window, which burst open, permitting the spectre the freedom of the night.

There have been many minor occurrences, bangs from bathrooms, the clinking of bottles and several times upturned glasses were found near small pools of whisky.

WHAT!!! Exorcise that varmint. There's no room in this book for a spirit that can't hold its liquor.

THE HOLE IN THE WALL
RICHMOND

Here is a story that has often been reported before so I shall just give the basic facts.

Kate Webster arrived at Liverpool from Ireland in or about 1849. She made her way from job to job, man to man and prison to prison. If there was any affection at all in Katie's body it was bestowed on her illegitimate son Johnny. Johnny was still very young when Kate appeared in splendorous Richmond in 1879 and worked as a live-in maid and skivvy for Mrs Julia Thomas, a widow of Park Road.

The two women did not get along from the start. If opposites attract this was the exception that proved the rule. Mrs Thomas was pernickety, fastidious and pedantic to a fault. Kate was a slovenly slut with a foul temper. It was because of Kate's temper that Julia Thomas justifiably feared for her life.

Kate Webster killed her mistress with a meat axe, boiled and roasted the dissected body, threw the head over Hammersmith Bridge and placed the rest of the body in a trunk, which with the help of an unsuspecting teenage boy was sent down the river to where it was later washed up. She then sold her mistress's furniture and clothes, festooned herself with her mistress's jewellery and attempted to sell some pots of dripping fat (don't even ask) to the landlord of the Hole in the Wall. She had to get caught and she did. Already suspicious, neighbours raised the alarm when two large pantechnicons arrived for Julia Thomas's furniture.

Kate fled to Ireland. She was traced, brought back, tried, convicted and hanged at Wandsworth prison. With the possible exception of Amelia Dyer, the Reading baby farmer, Kate Webster was probably Victorian England's most evil woman. The penny dreadfuls had a field day. It was probably one of those that initiated the ghost of a bony slovenly woman who heads up Park Road towards the Hole in the Wall, whispering, "Who will buy my dripping fat, my rich creamy dripping."

I do not know the flavour of human dripping. I don't doubt that Kate was eager to sell some. Her ghost however needs a pinch of salt added.

Lady St. Aubyn.

There is a house in Richmond named The Wick. It was built by a wealthy socialite, Lady St Aubyn, in 1775. The builders used the foundations of what once had been the Bull Inn. Many were the famous names of the day that found their way to The Wick. Sir Joshua Reynolds, who painted from his balcony next door was a regular visitor, as of course was the sovereign George III.

> Golden lads and lassies must
> Like chimney sweepers come to dust

All the rollicking merriment ended as the English aristocracy adopted a stricter and gloomier mode of behaviour, in public that is anyway.
It would seem the hostess with the mostess was loath to leave her delightful abode. Lady St Aubyn's spirit was witnessed for many years entering and leaving the old house.

There is little left of Richmond Palace other than the gatehouse. It was at the gatehouse however that Queen Elizabeth I died at 3 a.m. on March 24TH 1603. Legend dictates that although Good Queen Bess lay in a stupor for several days before her demise, her ghost, a type of spectral doppelganger, was not only strutting the palace but also barking out orders. There have been various reports of strange occurrences ever since but nothing that seems to stand up to any in depth scrutiny.

THE TALBOT INN
RIPLEY

The Talbot Inn stands at the end of Ripley High Street. It is surrounded by many other attractive old inns and the inevitable antique shops. The Talbot has been around since 1453 and had its heyday in that era, as of course did many of its near neighbours. Until fairly recent times the A3 London to Portsmouth road ran straight through the village. In coaching days Ripley's proximity to the capital made it an ideal spot for the final changing of horses.
It is a pity that antique shops have conglomerates in towns / villages like Ripley, picturesque as they may be. Other prime examples are Hungerford in Berkshire and Hartley Witney in Hants. They are both so overrun with antique shops it is difficult to buy a loaf of bread or a pint of milk.
Back to the Talbot which incidentally has an antiques business in its backyard. The inn has several claims to fame including the fact that Nelson stayed here with Lady Hamilton. A spinning wheel belonging to this exotic lady was once displayed in the bar as a conversation piece. I did not notice it on my last inspection but a charming and elegant restaurant is now

named the Emma Hamilton. The bars here are fine, beamed and with massive fires. There are also two of the country's earliest brass ale pumps. Unfortunately Café Braggs that has been around since the 17TH century has now been updated and the powder blue gives it the impression of a cafeteria. Being a traditionalist I believe in keeping Italian and Thai food out of pubs, but I do realise that a profit must be made.

OH! The ghost. I nearly forgot. It is a drunken coachman who fell to his death down the stairs. However he has not put in an appearance for over a decade.

Here's a little story about Ripley. It has nothing to do with ghosts and if you are not reading it, it is because I have decided to throw it out.

Once upon a time a Ripley village blacksmith threw a horse on its back so that he might shoe it more easily. Fine strong fellows were village blacksmiths of yore and this was not an unusual practice. However, the horse in question had a weak heart and died as it struck the ground. The blacksmith not realizing this proceeded to shoe the creature. When he had finished his work he stood back and flapped his apron to startle the horse into rising. This had no effect, so the blacksmith repeated the performance several times more. It was some minutes before he realised that he was flogging, sorry, flapping a dead horse.

Since that day residents of Woking and the surrounding villages have inferred that Ripley people are not too bright by doing apron flapping mannerisms in their presence. This action has led to many a brawl at local fairs.

CASTLE RESTAURANT HOTEL
(now CAFÉ ROUGE)
SUNBURY

This is a building that goes through a regular metamorphosis as far as its ownership is concerned. I can but wonder if the buildings suspected supernatural inhabitant puts pay to the potential living occupants. The ghostly inconvenience here is a young lady who frequents the ladies convenience, often entering through a locked door. The function of the room however has changed over the years. Formerly it was known as the Soldiers Room, so named because a troop of Cromwell's men was once billeted here. Being well in their cups a brawl started and a local barmaid was killed in the ensuing affray.

It is this poor young lady who has been frequently witnessed over the years. On one occasion a stench of evil invaded the premises. It may or may not have been connected with the poor maiden but it so affected the proprietor that he caused the room to be locked and barred. Not a great inconvenience one would have thought to lady who passes through doors and walls. Commonsense would therefore dictate that the evil stench was an entirely different entity. There have been no recent reports of anything supernatural or whether the offending door remains locked and bolted. When I arrived in early October 2001 the place was closed so I feel duty bound to pay another visit. The Café Rouge chain does fine service anyway. I did just wonder, as I noticed several small windowpanes broken on the second floor, if the young maid had finally escaped.

Or is that a bit too fanciful?

Here is a well known story concerning local Rossal House.

ROSSAL HOUSE
SUNBURY

It was known for years that Rossal House at Sunbury had a ghost, thought to be an old lady who had once been a domestic.

In 1910 the owner of the house was the famous electro-metallurgist, engineer and inventor Sherard Cowper-Coles. His wife, also a scientist, had reported seeing an unreal something. Scientists by their very nature are the last people prone to imagination. So Cowper-Coles decided to conduct some experiments. The first thing he did was to elicit the help of a friend. He called on Admiral Moore a member of the ghost club but also a very levelheaded man.

The two men photographed everywhere the wife had seen or sensed something strange. When developed, one photograph, that of a pink and white striped chintz armchair showed the grey head and features of what was thought to be an old lady. The two men were amazed; the chair had definitely been vacant when the picture had been taken.

The image on the photograph has never been identified. It has been my privilege to study this picture several times at length. There is no denying the face it is blatantly noticeable. The thing that struck me is that the image seems more like an 18TH century young man, complete with powdered wig than an old lady. After this length of time I feel sure that the spectre will never be identified.

CRICKETERS
(now FIELDER & FIRKIN)
SUTTON

What has happened to Sutton? I had not been there for years and when I visited in 2001 I could not find a familiar thing. That last statement is not quite true. The old cock struts still along the top of the High Street. I am sure the new shops and restaurants are modern, clean, efficient and in a characterless way, attractive. I am not mocking progress I just choose not to be part of it.

It is funny how the powers that be will bugger up your pubs but not your churches; no profit in it I suppose. There used to be a rather nice little story about St Nicholas here. In the 18TH century the mighty family of Gibson built a beautiful, if huge, mausoleum for five members of the family. In the 18TH century surgeons were keen to work on new dead cadavers; body snatching was profitable and rife. A Miss Gibson paid £500 for men to check the coffins once a month. It seems a little pointless to me, as any potential robbers would have 30 days a month to carry out their nefarious thefts. I believe that some type of ceremony prevailed into the 20TH century. It involved the local clergy and several of his henchmen emerging from the tomb once a year.

I set off down the High Street to find the Cricketers. Had I known how long it was I should have parked much lower down. I had found out that the number was once 246. After what seemed like an hour I was passing numbers like 76 and 84. I was however pleased to see that several of the old pubs had survived entirely in their original form. After a lot more tramping I finally came to 'The Cricketers'. Well anyway, to 'The Fielder and Firkin'. I should have effing well known. I entered, they were just opening and against my better judgement I asked if the premises were haunted. Everybody looked dumbfounded. I enquired no more.

Here's the legend. The Cricketers as one may well have guessed was on the perimeter of a cricket field. I see that there are still greens in the area. One of the first lady cricketers was struck on the head by the ball. Just feeling a little sickly she retired to the Cricketers where she later died, presumably from a brain haemorrhage.

For many a year a charming, refined and attractive lady cricketer's ghost frequented the bars. She was always attired in tight leather button up boots, a loose dark skirt, a long sleeved, stiff collared white shirt, club tie and white boater. Refined and genteel as the lady is, it did not stop a young barmaid from fainting when she suddenly came across her in the late 50's.

Dare I say it? Is this the first deceased cricketer to bowl a maiden over!

Whilst in Sutton I feel duty bound to mention Carshalton House that sits between the two towns.

CARSHALTON HOUSE
SUTTON

The prestigious Carshalton House was purchased by Dr John Radcliffe in 1713. Radcliffe was Queen Anne's personal physician and was constantly on call to nurse the good Queen's court. This being the case one questions the wisdom of purchasing such a property some distance from the Queen's bedside.

It seems to have been a rather unlucky choice for the Queen's messenger who was sent to Carshalton House to summon Radcliffe to his mistress's bedside. Being somewhat irritated by this 'command', the physician, showing good doctorly compassion and sensitivity, flung the messenger over the banisters to his death. Radcliffe was saved from the axeman's surgery by dying of a fever before his trial.

About a year later Sir John Fellowes, the new owner was met on the same stairs by a tax collector. Not being enamoured by this ridiculous institution, Sir John dispatched the revenue man by the same means as Dr Radcliffe had sent the Queens messenger. He pitched him over the balustrade breaking the poor fellows neck.

Unsurprisingly the flight of stairs is haunted by the shadowy form of a man. Whose shade it is, is down to the readers choice.

Is it a repentant Dr Radcliffe, a murdered Queen's messenger, an unrepentant Sir John Fellowes or a tax inspector with a broken neck? Personally I'd go for the tax inspector, they are forever with us.

THE WHEATSHEAF
THORNTON HEATH

Lovely old pub this, all timber clad on white, pity where it is situated. The Wheatsheaf stands with at least two other attractive old inns on one of the most frustrating roundabouts in London. When I arrived it was not open and it was raining hard. Preferring to get wet inside rather than outside, I gave up the ghost. I also didn't take a picture, which is rather a pity.

All the above balderdash is purely academic because the supposed ghost haunts without rather than within, it is a lady that spooks an adjacent duck pond. Whether or not this still exists I was too wet to affirm or deny. There are two stories, very similar, take your choice.

Story one.

In the 1600's or 1700's a king's daughter was murdered and thrown into the duck pond. Her shade has haunted the area ever since. Some say she knocks on the pub door for help.

Story two.

In the 1600's or 1700's the landlord's daughter was murdered and thrown into the duck pond. Her shade has haunted the area ever since. Some say she knocks on the pub door for help.

Personally I plumb for the landlords daughter I'm sure that if one of our kings daughters had been murdered the history books would have a record of it. The event would be made a lot of, i.e. the princes in the tower. Even some visiting foreign king's daughter would not go unmentioned.

Landlords' daughters however are two a penny; take it from one who has known hundreds in the last 40 years. But personally I do not think any self respecting ghost would habit this ultra busy neck of the woods.

THE DONKEY
TILFORD

The Donkey is easily missed, it is just off of the Farnham to Milford road twixt Tilford and Elstead. The exact spot is Charles Hill and the name of 'The Donkey' is to commemorate the donkeys that were kept here to help the horses and carts drag their way up the steep hill.

When I used the pub quite regularly in the mid-sixties the place abounded with exotic birds, monkeys, squirrels (red) and the inevitable donkey. On my latest visit in Autumn 2001 I noticed that two donkeys still remain.

The play area outside the inn was rumoured to be haunted by a donkey that was either starved or beaten to death by a cruel owner. This does not ring true to me, because, however sadistic a man may be, if donkeys are his living he is going to keep them in prime condition. It is like a taxi driver beating his engine to bits with a pickaxe handle. It just doesn't happen.

Suspecting that the ghostly donkey was not ill treated no way invalidates its existence. In the sixties the ring where the donkeys were tethered was still protruding from a wall. The then donkey in residence would wander all over the area even dropping in the bar for a pint. There was only one place that seemed to intimidate him. He would go nowhere near the ring in the wall. What could he see tethered there? One of his forefathers, sorry, foreasses?

THE GOLDEN GROVE
St. ANNES HILL, TWYNERSH Nr. CHERTSEY

Attractive old boozer this. One of my numerous jobs over the years was as a racecourse steward. The Golden Grove was a regular stop on the way home from Epsom. We were lucky enough to find a teetotaller who drove whilst the rest of us got 'hammered'. My daughters tell me that's the 'in' word. The Golden Grove has a ghost, though it is very seldom experienced. It is said to be a young girl who was murdered at the inn.

A separate ghost, yet another monk, walks dejectedly around a nearby pond. There are three ponds in the area and I am never sure which one it is supposed to be. One is now covered over and used as a reservoir. Yet another, I am told, disappeared when the M3 was constructed. The melancholy monk is suffering from a severe bout of conscience. When a nun from nearby St Anne's Convent threatened to expose their illicit love affair he buried her alive in some nearby sandpits.

There is now a marked walk around this beautiful beech wood, but the place where the poor girl was buried is not on the scheduled path. I had not been here for years but in late 2001, on a terrible day, I slipped and slid along a little known path. My way was blocked by fallen trees and I was only going my memory. I finally found it, a small ancient half brick covered springhead where centuries ago the nuns from St. Anne's drew their water.

On such a day this place reeks of remorse, suffering and sorrow. Thirty year ago on a fine day I brought my wife here, she was badly affected by the atmosphere and refused to go near. That was before I told her of the small bank behind where the nun was buried alive and of the deep begging sighs that come from it on certain nights. That is of course if you can hear them above the too nearby M3.

THE WHEATSHEAF
VIRGINIA WATER

It's a bit posh for me around here; Sunningdale, Wentworth, Ascot, some of the most palatial homes in the country. The famous lake was made in 1746 by the Duke of Cumberland, the 'Butcher of Culloden'. The lake with its ruins from Tripoli, its waterfall and the later added totem pole is well worth a visit. At the gates stands The Wheatsheaf, venue for this story, but in all honesty it could have happened anywhere.

Two firm friends met as schoolboys in one of England's best known public schools and as is the whim of young boys they cut their wrists and mingled blood and so became blood brothers. In a lengthy proclamation they both signed they swore to be friends even after death. And whomsoever should die first should contact the living one immediately after. After leaving school they both went their separate ways.

Many years later one of the boys, now a celebrated barrister, decided to take a weekend off and moved down to Virginia Water where he booked in at The Wheatsheaf. The first night whilst smoking his pipe by the fire he saw the images of his boyhood friend in the embers. For some reason he decided to go for a walk, much against the landlords advice. The weather was horrid but the barrister insisted.

As he walked around the lake he had a vision of a dark tunnel. From the tunnel emerged a train and through a window the barrister noticed two men fighting in a compartment. It was a terrible struggle. It was then that he noticed that one of the combatants was a middle-aged version of his boyhood pal. In his vision a knife was drawn and his friend was stabbed several times.

One assumes that the shaken barrister returned to his bed at The Wheatsheaf.

After the weekend the barrister returned to the city and by a chance in a million he came across his friends brother. Enquiring after his brother he was told that he had been murdered on a train in India. Further enquiries revealed that the poor man had met his death, late the previous Friday evening. I'll bet you've guessed it. That's right, at the precise time of the barrister's vision or dream.

I hate these bloody stories. This is yet another unverifiable variation of the 'vanishing hitch-hiker'. Personally I don't believe a word of it.

THE SHIP
WEYBRIDGE

In the 18TH century the Duchess of York was a very popular resident of Weybridge. Philanthropic and generous to a fault she was held in high esteem, so much so that a tall column that once marked Seven Dials in London was erected to her on the green. The column itself has quite a story to it, being uprooted from its original position by rioters because they believed gold lay underneath. Naturally it didn't, the fallen column was then bought by a Weybridge builder and left in his yard. After the death of the Duchess, Joseph Todd, landlord of the Ship Inn on the green, got up a local subscription to finance the resurrection of the column in her memory.

An eye to business had Joseph Todd. People flocked to see the new landmark, thirsty people that needed sustenance. What has all this got to do with a haunting? Very little, except Joseph Todd ran the old coaching inn when a series of events began.

In those far off days there was a chapel adjoining the inn and it was here that an ostler saw fit to end his days by hanging himself from one of the chapel's beams. The ostler's ghost was said to haunt the building. As suicide was very much frowned upon it did not take long for the local clergy to deconsecrate the building and close it down. The Ships landlord being less bothered about the odd spook, bought the property and amalgamated it into his inn. The lower floor making a fine billiard room and a vacant space in the roof became a small room. Frances D Stewart a talented local ghostwriter suggests that during the alterations the spectral ostler slipped in. If the regular sightings over the years are to be believed he certainly did.

THE GROTTO
WEYBRIDGE

The mighty palace of Oatlands stands no more. This beautiful abode was built by Henry VIII for his forth wife Anne of Cleves. But as our Anne did not last the distance the palace was appreciated by his fifth wife Catherine Howard. After the palace's demise the ruins were used for the construction of the Wey Navigational Canal.

The palace grounds lasted longer, they were laid out some 250 years ago by the Duke of Newcastle. He constructed a lake a mile long and spent £40,000 on a unique grotto. The Duke brought from Italy a father and two sons who laboured for 30 years adorning the grotto with shining crystals, minerals and horses teeth.

The Grotto public house was obviously named after the above construction. It is reputed to be the laundry house of the former Oatlands Palace. Many years ago the vast inglenook here held an open fireplace. One day a customer, pint in one hand, lent on the wall with the other.

"This wall is exceedingly hot," he stated to the landlord. The reason was only too obvious. On inspection it was revealed that the main beam holding the place up had been smouldering for years. The inglenook was bricked up for safety as was what reputedly lay behind, an underground passage to Oatlands Palace. This would seem to have silenced the disturbing footsteps, sighs and moans that had emanated from it for decades.

It would be impossible to leave Weybridge without mentioning Brooklands race track. But as it has been done oft times before I shall be brief.

BROOKLANDS
WEYBRIDGE

Racing tracks, both horse and motor, are well known for retaining spirits. The extreme human feelings of euphoria and despair may be in part responsible for this.

Motor racing at Brooklands began on a concrete track in 1907 and was abandoned just after the Second World War. Left to itself tufted grass pushed its way through the surface and later its vast space and geographical location made it ideal for every type of factory. Very little track remains today.

An indistinct racing machine has often been witnessed in what was once Railway Straight and seen to speed towards a hanger once known as The Vatican. A spiritual driver emerges, his features obscured by skullcap and goggles. A blur of racing overalls adorn the spectral body as the driver runs for cover. He then disappears before reaching his unknown destination. But who is this mysterious driver apparently fleeing for his life? Racing drivers as a species are as charismatic as they are fearless. With test pilots and bomb disposal experts they are a breed apart. A brotherhood so indelible that it is hardly surprising that their spirits should prevail after their emergence from the restricting confines of human form. There are two candidates that vie for the exalted position of Brooklands phantom driver. Both men met untimely deaths on the track.

In 1907 just after Brooklands opening Vincent Herman (Herman the German) was crushed to death by his overturned car.

Candidate two is the popular Percy Lambert, killed in October 1913. Percy met his maker whilst doing speed tests in his Talbot.

The identity of the overalled man in skullcap and goggles will never be known. You pays your money you takes your choice.

GRANTLEY ARMS
WONERSH

Wonersh is one of the most attractive villages in the county. Its ancient street meanders gracefully between its 15TH and 16TH century houses. It was for years an affluent cloth-weaving village and at one time imported woad from the continent.

The 15TH century Grantley Arms stands in the centre of the village. Its name is derived from Lord Grantley a local gentleman who once owned the building. This gentleman was a little too fond of gambling and legend states lost the inn to his servant at a game of poker.

The friendly ghost is that of a monk thought to be left over from when the site was a hostelry for travellers run by monks from a nearby monastery. Pleasant as the phantom brother may be he seemed to have an aversion to Christmas. Yuletide would seem to be the only time he appeared and then he would show his displeasure by pulling down the festive decorations. Hardly a Christian attitude one would have thought. Be that as it may an Irish live-in barmaid, of Catholic persuasion became a little peeved by the good brother's Christmas antics and decided on exorcism. I know little about exorcism, very few do, but I am pretty sure that the barmaid was not qualified and may have done more harm than good. The exorcism seems to have been successful, as the monk has not been recently seen. A bit harsh I think, the playful old gentleman meant no harm; he just got a little excited at Christmas.

A less attractive spirit at Wonersh was first brought to my notice by Andrew Green in his *Haunted Kingdom*.

The local church, dating from 1050 possesses some 15TH century brasses. They are displayed on the chancel floor. The brasses were dedicated to a local philanthropic family, the Eylots. Thomas and his wife, Henry and his wife and their combination of 23 children.

However there is something connected with the church that is neither benign, nor holy nor philanthropic. There would seem to have been an evil spirit here that took up residence in a couple of adjacent rooms that had been adapted into a study or den. In the 50's no one that rented the small apartment could stand the atmosphere. Tenants moved out with increasing rapidity. The feeling of depression verging on the suicidal seems to aptly describe the experience.